Turn Redunda
Opportunity

Practical books that inspire

The Ten Career Commandments
*Equip yourself with the 10 most important skills to move up
the career ladder*

Passing Psychometric Tests
*How to familiarise yourself with psychometric tests and
pass them every time*

Planning a Career Change
*How to take stock, change course and secure a better
future for yourself*

Rob Yeung's Insider Guide to Successful Interviews

howtobooks

Please send for a free copy of the latest catalogue to:

How To Books
3 Newtec Place, Magdalen Road,
Oxford OX4 1RE, United Kingdom
email: info@howtobooks.co.uk
www.howtobooks.co.uk

Turn Redundancy to Opportunity

*Proven techniques and programmes
for taking charge of your own future*

LAUREL ALEXANDER
3rd edition

howtobooks

First published by How to Books Ltd,
3 Newtec Place, Magdalen Road,
Oxford OX4 1RE, United Kingdom
Tel: 01865 793806 Fax: 01865 248780
email: info@howtobooks.co.uk
www.howtobooks.co.uk

© Copyright 2003 Laurel Alexander

First edition 1996
Second edition 2000
Third edition 2003

British Library Cataloguing in Publication Data.
A catalogue record for this book is available from
the British Library.

Cover design by Baseline Arts Ltd, Oxford

Produced for How To Books by Deer Park Productions
Typeset by Anneset, Weston-super-Mare, Somerset
Printed and bound by Cromwell Press, Trowbridge, Wiltshire

NOTE: The material contained in this book is set out in good
faith for general guidance and no liability can be accepted
for loss or expense incurred as a result of relying on particular
circumstances on statements made in the book. Laws and
regulations are complex and liable to change, and readers should
check the current position with the relevant authorities before
making personal arrangements.

Contents

List of Illustrations

Preface

to the third edition

Welcome to the third edition of the first book I ever wrote. A
lot of water has passed under the bridge since I had the idea
for a book which could help people rediscover their
confidence and find new opportunities in their working life.
I too have rediscovered new work opportunities in the last
three years following breast cancer!

The word 'job' is becoming obsolete. A job implies
boundaries, the parental company giving a job to those who
seek one and rewarding loyalty with promotion and salary
increases. In the workplace of today, it's the word 'work'
that is King. There may not be the kind of jobs our parents or
grandparents were familiar with, and there may not be the
traditional rewards offered. But there is plenty of work (and
financial remuneration) for anybody who is willing to look
for it and who can reinvent themselves to accommodate the
huge array of opportunities out there. Work can mean having
two or three strands of income. It can mean being employed
by a company to do one thing but being able to move on to
other roles. It can mean being self employed part-time and
PAYE for the rest of the time. It can mean approaching a
company on spec and creating work for yourself because
you're in the right place at the right time.

Being made redundant can happen to anyone – but it doesn't

mean you have to be a victim. So your job may have gone, your work load may have evaporated or been taken away, but that doesn't mean you have failed as a human being. Paid work is only one aspect of your life – you are multi-dimensional with many facets. Although we depend on paid work to put food in our belly and live our life as we choose, paid work is only a means to an end and losing some aspect of our paid work is not the end of you. You can choose your reaction to redundancy. Is a glass half full or half empty? Do you want to fall in a heap, hold onto your resentment and anger or would you rather stand tall and take control of your life?

We can't avoid losing a job or work through redundancy. What we can do is to have an eye on the future of the company we work for and know when the chips are down and we can continually update our skills so that we are a saleable commodity at any time.

To help you move forward, this book contains updated sections on selling yourself, using the internet to find work (including useful sites on the web), teleworking, becoming a consultant and new ways to work. Updating it has reminded me there are even more opportunities out there to take advantage of. So I'm off to find them as you will be soon. Good luck!

Laurel Alexander
laurel.alexander@ntlworld.com

$$\bigl(\,1\,\bigr)$$

Coping with the First Few Weeks

REACTING TO THE REDUNDANCY

'I'm sorry to have to tell you . . .'. There is no good way of being told that your job is no longer there for you to have! You may hear rumours for months before anything concrete happens. You may see other people go over a period of time. The company may become less busy. You wonder and worry.

During this time you may feel hopeful, frustrated and anxious. You may feel inclined to try even harder so that you won't be the one to go. Then, when the inevitable happens — you will feel stunned. You might go through a period of denial — a time when it doesn't sink in, you might have feelings of euphoria without the implications being acknowledged. You may experience elation at the thought of release from a job you hated. You may feel threatened over losing financial security. You may feel sad at the idea of losing touch with friends.

When it comes out of the blue, it is a huge shock and there is more likelihood of a grudge against the company. Why didn't they let anyone know?

Redundancy is now becoming an accepted word in our society. The structure of work is changing. Once we followed the traditional pattern of:

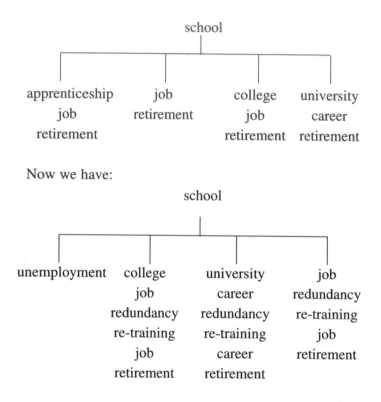

Now we have:

Redundancy is not necessarily linked to talent — it is usually about cost effectiveness and the restructuring of the business. But it may not feel like that when it happens to you.

We spend a lot of our waking hours at work. We gain the skills and knowledge for the job, we apply for the position, attend an interview and we then put time and effort into actually working.

Why do we work?

There are several reasons why we work — the main ones being power, status and money. We need to put a roof over our head and food in our mouth to survive and for this we need money. We may enjoy the trappings of luxury which indicate to others our worldly success. In our society, we tend to measure our worth by our possessions.

Many of us seek to express our identity through work and when our work is taken away — who are we? Where do we place ourselves in society? We often see ourselves through the eyes of others. When we believe others respect us, it means we have status. If we sense others are ridiculing us, we feel shame and anger and think of ourselves in a negative way. We believe that when we do our job of work, we are someone, others notice us, we have a place. When we have no work, we may feel lost, without purpose or not good enough to get by on the merit of our personality alone. We tend to judge ourselves and each other by what we have and what we do — not who we are.

We may seek to have power (financial or control over others) through our work. When this power is taken away from us, we may feel helpless.

Using career counselling

Some companies offer career counselling as part of the redundancy package. This may be a good option to take up or you could decide to use an external careers counsellor. The service may offer psychometric testing for assessing your interests, personality and skills together with guidance on refocusing your career direction and on training opportunities. At the very least, companies should offer you job-hunting time.

SAYING GOODBYE

The last few days

Some companies request that you leave the premises immediately you receive redundancy notice so that you don't affect other staff or do anything detrimental to the company. Most companies, however, require some notice to be worked. This can be difficult. Motivation is low and feelings are high. You don't feel inclined to do your job which will make money for the company which is rejecting you. You may experience the bitterness of the 'why me?' syndrome and want it to be someone else.

The time between when you know and when you go is bound to be tense. Ideally just working out your notice to the best of your ability and making the best of a bad situation is the easiest way through a very difficult situation. You may dream about taking your redundancy money and blowing it — for the first time in your life, you may have more money than you've ever had. Dream a little! And it's never too early to start looking for another job.

◆ *Checkpoint*
   It may be worth while negotiating to take a lump sum and leave rather than work out your notice.

Beginning to network

It is a good idea to begin developing contacts (networking) before you finally leave the company (or when you begin to hear rumours). Colleagues and management in particular can be useful. Networking is an invaluable key to your next job. Don't be shy of telling people you've been made redundant.

Be a floater

Accessing and sharing information with others.

Get a mentor

The definition of a mentor is someone who coaches and gives advice. To acquire a mentor you need to be seen to have qualities which suggest you are going somewhere.

Get sponsors

A sponsor is someone who promotes you to others. Being well perceived and possessing a high level of visibility are vital.

Network your boss

Assisting your boss to strengthen his/her network is likely to result in opportunities for you. Identify your boss's route of networking and get visibility on this route. Networking your boss to key personnel (inside and outside your company) should connect you with some vital people and give you extra opportunities.

◆ *Networking project*
   Draw up an organisational chart adding the names and job titles for your organisation or department. Who could be of help to you?

DEALING WITH LOSS

Self-assessment

Since being told you have been made redundant, are you experiencing:

a lack of personal fulfilment	loss of status
worry about your income	loss of independence
a change in lifestyle	lack of community support
fear about change	anxiety about decision making
an inability to share feelings	family discord
concurrent life crisis e.g. divorce	excessive activity
depression (apathy, fatigue, withdrawal)	feelings of alienation
anger	powerlessness
guilt	shame
nervous anxiety	physical ailments or illness
self pity	confusion and mood swings

A combination of any of these could indicate that you are going through the grieving process. This process is where we honour the loss of job, status and friends amongst other things.

What do we lose?

Self esteem

Our sense of who we are, and our security surrounding our place in society, as defined through work, can feel threatened. We may feel shaky about our skills and knowledge. Weren't we good enough for the job? Are we good enough to get another job?

Dignity

Most of us develop a sense of pride in what we do for a living. There is a sense of ownership and attachment to what we have produced. When this living is taken away from us, we see the beliefs and values which we have attached to our work disappear.

Personal fulfilment

Work can provide a great deal of satisfaction. It affirms what we can do and what we know. It can affirm that we are needed. When work is no longer there, we may find it hard to find pleasure in more basic achievements.

Status

There may be feelings of shame attached to the label of redundant. Although nowadays there is more sympathy, there is still an ingrained sense of shame in the belief that we are not wanted. We take it as a personal affront, men in particular believing their identity is linked to their work.

Income

This is a major loss. If we don't have money, how will we eat, keep a roof over our heads and pay the bills? Linked to this is the loss of luxuries — the car, the holiday, the meals out. What will happen to the savings?

Independence

For many of us, work represents financial independence. It

may also represent independence from the role of parent or carer. Work may be seen as a place where we can be expressive and free.

Lifestyle

Certain lifestyles can be connected with many jobs, e.g. sales or management. Overnight stays, company cars or entertaining are some of the perks we may lose when made redundant.

Property

When faced with redundancy, one of the major fears is the loss of our home. It may be that our home is linked directly with our job, e.g. caretaking or if we work for a bank. Even if our home is not directly linked, there is the threat of it being taken away if we don't keep up the mortgage repayments.

What complicates loss?

Lack of community support

One of the first questions we normally ask someone we first meet is 'what do you do'? If at that point we are not working, we may feel uncomfortable with this question. It is indicative of our society that we label each other by our work.

Change

Part of the human condition is a need to feel safe and secure. We do not mind change so much if we are in control, but when external circumstances force our hand, we tend to react with hostility and fear.

Anxiety about making decisions

When we are made redundant, we face the unknown. We

have to make decisions about ourselves, what we want and how we are going to get it. Many of us fear making decisions because we don't want to make the wrong ones — so we don't make any and end up feeling lost and frustrated.

Inability to share feelings
Redundancy invariably produces an emotional reaction and emotions can be difficult to handle, especially if there is a lack of support or acceptance around us. If we are not happy with our own emotions, we tend to reject the emotions of others.

Family discord
At the time of losing our job, we may already be experiencing difficulties in our personal relationships. Redundancy may make these communication problems even more pronounced.

Presence of concurrent life crises
Sometimes life seems to empty all the negative out at once. It may be that we are experiencing problems in other areas of our life and then just to cap it all along comes redundancy.

The grieving cycle

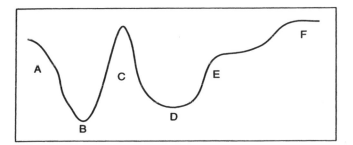

Fig. 1. The grieving cycle.

A The pattern of **life prior to redundancy**. During this time we may be advancing in our work and getting a sense of achievement. Or maybe we are hating our work or feeling uncomfortable with those we work with.

B The **loss and shock** due to redundancy with maybe a temporary numbness or disbelief. Some people may react with excessive activity, others with depression. There may be a feeling of unity with others in the company at the sense of loss. There may be feelings of alienation. The world stands still when we hear that we are being made redundant. We don't want to believe our world is falling apart. We don't want to believe that someone doesn't want us. We don't want to believe we are dispensable. We go blank. We may stay blank. We don't talk about it. We may immerse ourselves in activity so we don't think about it. We just can't believe it. Redundancy happens to other people. Not us. But it has happened and we have to deal with it somehow. We feel apart, alone, separate. We may not want to tell our family and friends — they have jobs, we don't. We may feel separate from colleagues at work who still have their jobs.

C **Emotional reaction** such as anger, powerlessness, guilt. We hang our heads, we hide away in shame. The great British stiff upper lip shows itself. Don't cry or shout, don't lose control because you've lost your job. Feeling powerless and out of control of our employment is a frightening state. We feel small, helpless and vulnerable, like a child again. Anger at your boss, at the company, the managing director, God, the government.

Underlying anger which you feel at yourself may be redirected at your family. Anger turned inwards against the self can often turn into depression and apathy. Low self esteem and lack of confidence may evolve. Internal tension such as nervous anxiety may show itself. Psychosomatic ailments such as backache, headache or an illness may manifest. We feel self pity. With the confusion and mood swings that come with redundancy, we may not feel like exposing ourselves to the act of love-making.

D Onset of the **grieving process** where the reality of redundancy is experienced.

E **Change** where the loss is accepted and the idea of re-employment becomes a reality.

F **Rebuilding** a new working life.

Guidelines for healthy grieving

- to accept my sense of loss
- to let my feelings flow
- not to try to replace the loss immediately
- to let myself be with the pain of loss
- to talk to safe people about my feelings
- to take good care of myself
- to involve myself with meaningful activity
- to have fun
- to take the time I need.

Working with anger

Anger is a primary emotion following redundancy. It is fuelled by a sense of frustration and powerlessness. It may also be a cover for fear and anxiety about the future.

Getting angry helps us to:

- discover what happened and what is happening to us
- set limits where necessary
- grieve for our losses
- get our needs met
- discover what is beneath our anger
- be assertive
- get things off our chest.

Repressed anger can cause:

- resentment
- self pity
- stress
- anxiety
- depression
- sadness
- lack of concentration
- physical illness.

Choices in handling anger

- smother it and experience numbness
- hold it in until it becomes resentment
- let it fester away inside until it becomes a physical illness
- displace the anger and cover it with work, eating, drugs or alcohol
- express it appropriately.

Expressing the anger appropriately

- grieve
- do some physical activity e.g. exercise
- punch a cushion
- scream into a pillow
- scream in your car with the windows wound up
- write an 'open letter' stating exactly how you feel (then keep it or burn it)
- tear up newspapers, magazines or the phone book
- cry
- take control and take action e.g. plan your job search.

Self evaluation of anger

1. Do you believe you have a right to be angry?

2. If you do express anger, how do you do it? Are you aggressive, assertive, stubborn, complaining, rebellious?

3. Identify what you feel is being hurt and threatened by your anger.

4. List specific examples of your behaviour that indicate you can express anger in a healthy way.

Making friends with fear

Fear can be a debilitating emotion. But it is natural and it is better to make a friend of fear and to work with it than to be afraid of fear itself.

We may fear:

- the loss of purpose and meaning in our lives
- the loss of status

- the loss of job and material possessions
- the unknown
- unpredictability
- the loss of control
- looking foolish
- change
- loss of financial security
- making decisions
- changing a career
- asserting oneself
- being interviewed
- making a mistake
- rejection
- success
- failure
- being vulnerable
- loss of image
- disapproval
- helplessness
- filling in forms

Questions we ask ourselves

- How will I financially survive?
- Am I too old to get another job?
- What will my friends say?
- Will my home be taken away?
- What will the neighbours say?
- Who else will want me?
- What will happen to me?
- How do I tell my partner?
- How do I pay my bills?

Low self esteem

When we experience low self esteem, we may:

- fear rejection
- fear failure
- need to be perfect
- appear incompetent
- have a negative self-image.

As our self esteem increases, we:

◆ become more confident
◆ express feelings
◆ take risks
◆ act more assertively.

COPING WITH THE FIRST FEW DAYS

Lazing around

We are so used to 'doing', we may find it hard to let go. The first few days or weeks after you have finished work, you may feel lost — without purpose. Try to use this time to create some space to have fun, to let go. It may be hard for the mind to stop, but it can be helpful to slow down and allow a sense of positive freedom to enter.

Catching up

You could use some of the time to catch up on those odd jobs. This may help with a sense of achievement and usefulness. You could.

◆ finish some household chores
◆ catch up on paperwork
◆ do some DIY
◆ see old friends
◆ indulge your hobbies.

Nurture yourself

If we have lost our job, we can spend a lot of time mentally beating ourselves up. We forget to forgive ourselves, to take care of ourselves. If our best friend had lost their job, we would listen to them, be with them, help to cheer them up. So maybe we need to treat ourselves as our own best friend. We need to have fun, to nurture ourselves. Maybe you could:

◆ visit some interesting places

◆ buy yourself something special you can afford

◆ listen to a positive and motivational tape

◆ meditate.

Being with family and friends

Emotional support from family and partners is vital for you to feel valued and accepted. It is good to have special people who will listen to you.

Your thought process

Our thought process gives rise to our reality in life. If we have negative beliefs, we experience negative outcomes in life. When we experience positive self talk, we then have a good chance of experiencing the best that life can offer.

One way in which we can identify negative beliefs is by managing four different parts of our nature that send us messages:

◆ **The critic**
   'What a disappointment you are —'
   'You can't provide for your family —'

◆ **The perfectionist**
   'You should —'
   'You must —'

◆ **The worrier**
   'What if —'
   'We won't have a roof over our heads —'

◆ **The victim**
'I'll never be able to get another job —'
'No one wants me —'

We may have further negative beliefs that come from our past
such as:

◆ I must not show anger
◆ I must keep a stiff upper lip
◆ I can't handle rejection
◆ They don't appreciate me
◆ It's my fault
◆ I must not seem vulnerable
◆ I can't handle uncertainty
◆ They've got no right to get rid of me
◆ I'm not good enough
◆ I must always be working.

Using mind power

You can use the power of your mind to help improve your
confidence, for example:

1 Create a mental image for your doubting side:
   e.g. a thin, black creature pointing accusingly.

2 Create a mental image for your reinforcing side:
   e.g. an all wise male dressed in white with a flowing
   beard.

3 What negative messages is your doubting side saying?
   e.g. 'no one wants your skills'.

4 What positive messages can your reinforcing side say?
   e.g. 'my skills are useful and I keep adding to them'.

List your positives

This is the time to be upbeat about yourself and your achievements, for example:

- 6 x qualities I like about myself
- 2 x times I have felt loved
- 2 x times I have been congratulated
- 2 x difficulties I handle well
- 4 x responsibilities I shoulder successfully.

Beginning your new routine

Although it's nice to have the odd lay in, you need to get yourself into a constructive routine as soon as possible. You could:

- get up at a regular time
- exercise
- network with colleagues and friends
- socialise
- improve your image
- reorganise your finances
- do voluntary/community work
- get out and about
- write your CV
- get in touch with agencies
- redefine personal goals
- return to study
- redefine career goals.

CHECKLIST FOR THE FIRST FEW WEEKS

1 See redundancy as a positive opportunity for change.
2 Allow yourself time to grieve and say goodbye.

3   Express your anger appropriately.

4   Write out your feelings.

5   Can your life or health cover continue after you leave?

6   Put your financial package in a high interest account.

7   Could you negotiate a lump sum and leave rather than work out your notice?

8   Organise networking contacts before you leave.

9   Keep busy.

10 Look after yourself.

11 Have some fun.

2

Handling Your Finances

When you are made redundant, there are payments to which you are entitled.

Your employer should pay:

- any wages you are owed
- holiday pay (for holidays you are entitled to but haven't taken)
- in lieu of notice if you have not been given the proper period of notice
- redundancy payment.

Your redundancy package is likely to include **financial compensation**. At this point, it may be tempting to go out and blow the lot. The sensible short-term policy would be to put it into a high-interest account in the building society or bank, dream a little, then after some distance is put between your turbulent emotions and your money — take rational action.

Redundancy payments under the statutory scheme are not taxable. An employee may be entitled to a redundancy payment if they were dismissed from their job and:

- have been continuously employed in the job for at least two years since the age of 18
- the dismissal was for redundancy; and
- they were not covered by any of a number of specific

exclusions, eg:
- people 65 and over; or
- a lower age if the employer has a lower retirement age;
- people working outside Great Britain; and
- people who unreasonably refuse an offer of suitable alternative work.

If the employer does not make the redundancy payment at the time of dismissal, you must claim the payment in writing within six months of the date of dismissal. The amount of a redundancy payment is a multiple of your normal weekly gross pay, depending on your age and length of continuous employment with the employer.

Look for DTI employment legislation booklet PL808 on 'Redundancy Payments'.

If you require further guidance about statutory redundancy entitlement, consult a Citizens Advice Bureau or seek independent legal advice. Any dispute about entitlement should be referred to an employment tribunal. Redundancy booklets can be ordered from:

DTI Publications
Tel: 020 7215 6024
Website.dti.gov.uk/publications

If you have lost your job and your former employer owes you money which the company cannot pay because of insolvency, the Employment Department may be able to settle the debts, or part of them. Self-employed people do not qualify. The main debts you can claim include: any wages you are owed, holiday pay and compensation for financial loss you may have suffered by not being given a proper period of notice or pay in lieu of notice.

Checkpoints for your redundancy package

- ◆ Can you retain your company car for a while?
- ◆ Could you purchase your company car at a favourable rate?
- ◆ Can you negotiate the continuation of life or health insurance cover for a short time after you leave?
- ◆ Is there payment for career counselling or outplacement assistance?
- ◆ Are you owed holiday pay?
- ◆ What happens to your pension?

Using your redundancy money

Make your money work for you:

- ◆ pay off any hire purchase
- ◆ don't rush into buying a business
- ◆ don't take the first person's advice that you speak to
- ◆ don't be speculative
- ◆ check to see if your loan agreement has any insurance cover against unemployment
- ◆ put your money into a high interest account until you have had the best advice.

Organising your personal budget

- ◆ keep outgoings minimal
- ◆ look at your expenditure
- ◆ you may be able to take a private pension from age 50
- ◆ your work pension is likely to be frozen

◆ keep your life insurance going.

Using the benefit system

Your redundancy payment does not affect your entitlement to unemployment benefit. For advice and information on benefits, talk to a claimant adviser at the Jobcentre.

Facts about Job Seekers Allowance (JSA)
JSA is paid if you are under 65 (for men) or under 60 (for women) and not working (but are capable, available and actively seeking work), or working on average less than 16 hours a week. Further facts include:

◆ If you have been paying NI contributions you may be able to get contribution-based JSA. If you are on a low income you may get income-based JSA, even if you have not paid NI contributions. Income-based JSA is based on how much the law says you need to live on.

◆ Redundancy payments and other money you get when a job ends may affect JSA and the date you can get JSA from.

◆ If you take voluntary early retirement you may not get JSA straight away. If you get an occupational or personal pension, it may reduce your JSA.

◆ Men aged 60 to 64 who do not want to sign on at the Jobcentre every 2 weeks can claim income support instead.

◆ You cannot usually get JSA if you are studying full-time. If you are one of a couple that are both full-time students and one of you is responsible for a child, you may be able to get JSA during the summer vacation. For more information about how studying affects JSA and other benefits, see leaflet GL19: School-leavers and students. If

MONTHLY OUTGOING	AMOUNT	MONTHLY INCOMING	AMOUNT
rent/mortgage		salary — spouse	
council tax		unemployment benefit	
water rates		building society interest	
house/contents insurance		child allowance	
life insurance		severance pay	
electricity		retirement income	
gas		share dividends	
telephone		other	
car			
public transport			
savings			
food			
newspapers/subscriptions			
your clothes			
children's clothes			
cigarettes			
birthdays/Christmas			
meals out/alcohol			
holidays			
loans			
TV rental/licence			
household			
credit cards			
HP			
childcare			
health insurance			
other			
Total		Total	

Fig. 2. Your budget plan.

you are studying part-time, but are still available for and actively seeking work, you may be able to get JSA. This will also depend on the number of hours you study and your other circumstances. If you are aged 25 or over and have been unemployed for 2 years or more, you may be able to do a full-time employment-related course for up to a year and still get JSA. You may be able to do an Open University course and still get JSA.

Other useful benefits include:

◆ Back to Work Bonus
◆ Business Start Up
◆ Budgeting Loans
◆ Council Tax Benefit
◆ Employment on Trial
◆ Income Support
◆ Job Grant
◆ Mortgage Interest Run-On
◆ New Deal
◆ Working Families' Tax Credit

Internet hotspot
Deptartment for Work & Pensions
www.dwp.gov.uk/lifeevent/benefits/index.htm

Checkpoints

◆ Doing voluntary work should not affect your benefit as long as you are still actively searching for work.
◆ If you have a mortgage, see your building society or bank to discuss rescheduling your repayments.

YOUR LOW COST OR NO COST LIFESTYLE

Gardening Tidying up and weeding cost nothing. If you're in the season of cuttings, ask your friends and neighbours for a free sample.

Decorating and home furnishings Four tins of paint and you can transform a room. If you don't want to paint, give the paintwork a good washdown instead, cost — only soap and water. Don't always think just about the purchase price of an appliance, consider how much it costs to run. Consider energy saving around the home. Consider buying your furnishings from auctions.

Your car If you are thinking of buying another car, consider how much it will depreciate in the first year and what else you could do with that money. A smaller powered engine attracts a lower vehicle road tax rate. The higher the gear the lower your fuel consumption. The heavier the car the more fuel it will take to move it. If waiting in a queue for longer than two minutes turn off your engine to conserve energy. Driving at lower speeds will reduce fuel consumption.

Food and drink Invest in a home brew kit. The outlay is minimal and you can have lots of fun preparing brews of cider, wine and beer. If you don't want to buy the ready made kits, you can make home brew from almost anything in your garden or kitchen cupboard. Ask your friendly greengrocer for the vegetables or fruit they normally throw away. Try not to spend too much on convenience foods. Don't be put off by plain packaging if the product is cheap.

Entertainment and holidays Go for a walk in the country, visit the local pub for a drink and a snack, have fish and chips. Visit a museum, browse in a music or book shop, take a scenic drive, go to the beach, walk on a scenic path in the park. Hiring a video is cheaper than going to the cinema. Look out for free concerts advertised in the local paper. When eating out a set menu is cheaper than à la carte. Consider late availability holidays from travel agents or a house swap for a cheap holiday. Rent a house with friends for the summer break.

Clothes   Oxfam do a great deal on business suits these days. Alternatively wait for the sales, have a swop shop with friends or, if handy with a needle and thread, revamp your own.

Keep fit   Run round the block, walk everywhere, exercise with a friend.

Philosophy   Self expression, self respect, a sense of purpose, — none of these cost anything to nuture in yourself.

DEFINING YOUR NEEDS AND WANTS

It is easier to look at what others want and need instead of looking inside ourselves. We are often taught to ignore our own needs and focus on others. Society and conditioning contribute to what we believe we must have in order to be happy. Of course we need a roof over our heads and food in our mouths, but there are many appendages we believe we cannot survive without.

Needs are associated with what humans require for their physical survival. According to the psychologist Abraham Maslow, there are five levels of human needs:

- ◆ Physiological needs — food, water, sleep, oxygen
- ◆ Safety needs — shelter, stable environment, income

- Belongingness — support from others, a sense of belonging
- Esteem needs — self-respect, skill, status, a sense of accomplishment
- Self actualisation — fulfilment of your potential in life, self determination.

Projects

1. Make two separate lists — the ten things you most want to do and the ten things you most often do. Compare.

2. Spend a whole day paying attention to how many times you say 'I want' or 'I need'. What do you want and need?

3. Take ten blank postcards and write on each card 'What I need is —' and complete the phrase without judgement. Take another ten postcards and write on each card 'What I want is —' and complete the phrase without judgement. Prioritise each section. What do they tell you?

REDEFINING YOUR MATERIAL VALUES

Most of us seek attachment to the external world via money, our home, a car and other possessions. We believe that our survival depends on us having these things. We believe that our possessions are a gauge of who we are and whether we are accepted by others.

Some of us are ruled by what we see as the importance of money: 'others will like me if I have lots of money' or 'If I had more money, I could do more things/buy more things and then I would be happy'.

♦ We are fearful about money. If we don't have enough, we are afraid that we won't have what we need. If we are rich, we are afraid of losing it. We may have lots of money but feel guilty about it or we may have less and feel resentful about it. In the area of work and money you may have to be willing to take risks. If you do only what you think you should in order to earn a living, then you won't be listening to your inner voice that tells you what you really need to do. Our hopes and fears around money tend to come from our conditioning as seen through the eyes of our first family as well as what we as a society tend to view as the 'norm' e.g. owning a car (or two), and an annual holiday abroad.

Self-assessment

1. Reflect on the things you believe you need to have in your life and list ten things that you feel are indispensible to your well-being.

2. Tick those needs you feel are not being met right now.

3. List ten things you most want. Brainstorm without judgement.

4. Tick those wants that you feel you deserve. Compare how deserving you feel with how difficult you think your wants are to obtain.

5. Compare the two lists of wants and needs. On a separate sheet, put your two lists in descending order of importance. Note any changes.

In summary, if you organise **sensible budgeting**, money should be no problem. You may have to tighten the belt a little and not indulge in luxuries as you used to. But the good times will come back with patience and forethought. You may see your redundancy money as a safety net, you may use it to pay off some debt or it might give you the opportunity to make changes you've always wanted — and change is what redundancy is offering you.

$$\boxed{3}$$

Making Changes

COPING WITH CHANGE

Most of us have a need to feel in control. When we instigate change, we feel in control, but redundancy happens to us — outside of our control. This can produce a reaction of feeling angry and overwhelmed. We need to regain some sense of control in order to cope with the enforced change. We can do this by:

- managing our time to explore and plan our life
- learning how to relax and nurture ourselves
- positive thinking
- looking after our health.

Other ways of helping ourselves cope with change include:

- getting as much information as possible about our situation
- learning the skills of decision making and goal setting
- networking
- expressing our feelings constructively.

There is nothing so constant as change, the saying goes. Change can bring fear and uncertainty but it can also bring fresh challenge and new opportunities.

Try completing — truthfully — the chart in Figure 3 and then make an effort to increase the good elements and cut down on the bad.

	Yes	Sometimes	No
Physical well-being			
I have a balanced daily diet of proteins and fibre			
My weight is appropriate for my age and height			
I drink at least two litres of water per day			
I drink no more than two pints of beer or two measures of spirits/wine daily			
I don't smoke cigarettes or cigars			
I take care of my appearance			
I walk at least two miles a day			
I take part in non-competitive games or sport on a weekly basis			
I practise deep breathing/relaxation			
I spend regular time in the fresh air			
Mental and emotional well-being			
I have close friends			
I ask for support when I need it			
I give myself treats			
I have interests which enable me to learn new skills			
I have a sense of self-direction			
I have a good image of myself			
I can let go appropriately			
I am emotionally secure			

Fig. 3. Looking after yourself.

LOOKING AFTER YOUR HEALTH

Coping with the transition of change isn't easy. Although redundancy can give us a positive outcome, the process of arriving at that outcome can cause us stress. Therefore we need to have at our fingertips all the coping strategies we can, including stress and time management.

Both of these techniques have much to offer other areas of our lives as well as in career management. When we have a secure base within, we are in better shape to go out into the world. Looking after our mind and body, being selective over how we use our time, cultivating a positive attitude and exploring our work values and motivations can only have a beneficial effect on us and our career development.

Managing your stress

Stress is caused not by an event, but by your response to the event. If you can control your levels of response, you can control stress. If you cannot change the environment, then you must change yourself and the perception of the event. Psychologists have suggested there are two types of responses to stress:

◆ Type A — Impatient, aggressive, driven, distorted sense of time, fast talker and mover. High risk of heart problems. The positive interpretation of this type of response could be — expressive, in control and sociable.

◆ Type B — Relaxed, unhurried, non-competitive and non-aggressive. The negative of this type of response could be — overcontrolled and inhibited.

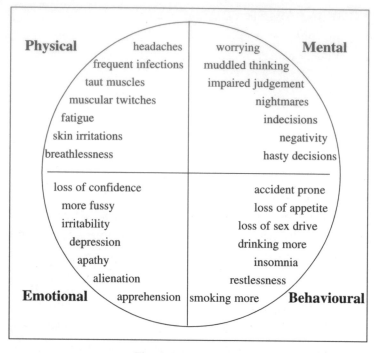

Physical headaches
frequent infections
taut muscles
muscular twitches
fatigue
skin irritations
breathlessness

worrying **Mental**
muddled thinking
impaired judgement
nightmares
indecisions
negativity
hasty decisions

loss of confidence
more fussy
irritability
depression
apathy
alienation
Emotional apprehension

accident prone
loss of appetite
loss of sex drive
drinking more
insomnia
restlessness
smoking more **Behavioural**

Fig. 4. Signs of stress.

Developing your security zones

Security zones are places, things or routines in your life which represent security and safety to you. They are areas of your life which are under your control or don't change.

What are your security zones?

Home

A favourite chair

Walking the dog

Watching old films

Talking to friends

Sunday outings

Beach

Comfy clothes

Reading

Hobbies

Holidays

The hairdresser

Friday night down the pub

The morning cup of tea

Your favourite restaurant

Watching cartoons

A favourite room

The weekly shopping

Pets

Gardening

Eating

Sleeping

Having a bath

Cuddling

Using relaxation techniques

Relaxation exercise

You could get someone to read this exercise to you or you could record it for yourself, speaking clearly and slowly. Wear loose clothing and find yourself a quiet, safe space where there are no telephones and you won't be interrupted. Sit in a comfy chair, lie on the bed or rest on the floor, with or without a cushion. The idea is not to go to sleep, but to change your level of consciousness to a more relaxed and peaceful state.

When you feel comfortable, close your eyes and become aware of your body, starting with your scalp. Feel your scalp relaxing, imagine someone is soothing back your hair and stroking all the tension away. Relax the forehead, raise the eyebrows and then lower them again, feeling the frown ease away. Feel the eyelids gently shut. Relax the facial muscles. Unclench the jaw. Wiggle the jaw from side to side and feel the tension ease away. Your tongue should be behind the lower teeth. Let your attention go to your throat and neck. Feel the tension easing. Imagine all the tension in your forehead and scalp going out of the base of your skull into infinity.

Move your attention down to your upper chest, feeling the muscles relax. Move your shoulders down and back, feel them relaxing into the chair, bed or floor. Move your attention to your left shoulder, relaxing the upper arm and the lower arm, feeling the tension flow into your left hand and out of your fingertips into infinity. Move your attention over to your right shoulder, relaxing the upper arm and the lower arms, feeling the tension flow into your right hand and out of your fingertips into infinity. Move your attention round to your back as it rests against the chair, floor or bed. Feel the tension easing in your upper back and your lower back. Feel the tension from your forehead, scalp and back drain down your spine and out of the small of your back into infinity. Move your awareness round to your stomach and feel the muscles relax and ease.

Relax your upper thighs and your calves, feeling the tension in your hips and legs flow into both feet and out of your soles into infinity. You are becoming more and more relaxed. More and more peaceful. There is nothing to do, nothing to change, just relax — relax — relax — relax.

Deep breathing

When you are in a stressed state, the breathing becomes shallow. Deep breathing can help to relax and focus the thoughts. The idea is to expand the stomach and rib cage, thereby using your entire lung capacity. You **inhale slowly and deeply** and **exhale even more slowly**.

Lie down in a comfortable position and place one hand either side of the stomach, fingers facing each other. As you inhale, make a concentrated effort to raise the stomach and feel your fingers expand. Slowly exhale completely. Now inhale for a count of five and exhale for a count of six. Do this five more times. Still with your hands on your stomach, inhale for a count of three, feeling the stomach rise. Now place one hand either side of your rib cage, fingers facing in. Continue to inhale for a count of seven, feeling the rib cage expand outwards. Now slowly exhale completely for a count of ten. Repeat five times.

Further stress-busting ideas

meditate	laugh	cry	slow down
do yoga	exercise	shout	make love
shrug it off	punch a cushion	write it out	detach from it

Face, head and neck massage

Self massage can help relieve muscle tension, easing the muscles into movement and stimulating the blood supply. Any one of the following may help ease tension:

1 Close your eyes and place the palms of each hand over your eye socket. You should find the result very restful.
2 Move your fingers along the edge of your skull from your ears towards the spine, and continue down the spine as far as you can. Then push the back neck muscles up towards your head.
3 Put your left hand on your right shoulder and roll the back muscle up and forward. Repeat with your right hand on your left shoulder.
4 Move your scalp over your skull with your fingertips.

Eating the healthy way

We are not talking diet but an all round healthy eating regime, which, without you even trying, will be low in fat, high in fibre and should result in your being the right weight.

Ultimately a little of what you fancy does you good. There is no point in eating and drinking all the right things if you die of boredom along the way. A general guide could be:

- limit your intake of salt
- bananas, kiwi fruit, celery, grapes, lettuce, cinnamon, barley, brewer's yeast, oats, and basil are good soothers for stress levels
- increase your intake of low fat foods such as pasta, oily fish, bread, white meat, vegetables, fruit and salad
- minimise intake of sugar and refined carbohydrates
- if you have low blood sugar, you will need a high protein/low carbohydrate diet with small, frequent meals
- alcohol, antibiotics, coffee, tea and sleeping pills destroy vitamin B which is vital to the nervous system
- garlic, pumpkin seeds and sunflower seeds are good pep-ups
- avocado, lentils, raspberries and spinach are good for fatigue
- ginseng is a well known nutrient for stress (Siberian for the mind and Korean for the physical)
- calcium, magnesium, zinc, vitamin B and C complex are beneficial for the nervous system.

Rest and recreation

We all need to play, sleep, dream and slob out from time to time. This provides us with the space to recharge our batteries and build up our reserves. It may even be, in these quiet times, that creative solutions to our problems occur.

USING POSITIVE THINKING

There is now plenty of scientific documentation demonstrating how the mind affects the body. When under severe or prolonged stress, the immune system doesn't function at optimum and it is the immune system which keeps infection and illness at bay. If we are in a negative emotional or mental state, this can affect our physical well-being, thereby leading to disease.

A healthy mind is equal to a healthy body — the more positive we feel, the more healthy we are. The power of positive thinking not only affects our bodies, but also our experiences in life. What we think and how we feel produce the choices we make available to ourselves. From these choices, we make decisions and from these come our life experiences. Two techniques used to access positive thinking are **visualisations** and **affirmations**.

Visualisation

To visualise is to use our mind's eye. We can see in our mind a person close to us even though we are not with them, we can visualise our favourite food or replay our favourite film.

Exercise

Sit or lie down in a quiet, comfortable place and go through your relaxation and deep breathing exercise. Try to visualise what your stress looks like, e.g. a tightly squeezed cloth, sharp teeth or turbulent waves. Now imagine the opposite, e.g. gently rippling silk, smooth curves or still water.

Affirmations

Affirmation means 'to make firm'. An affirmation is a short statement, written or spoken, which affirms the positive. It is always worded in the present and reinforces the good that you want.

Exercise

Take a sheet of paper and write down some positive affirmations, e.g. relax, calm down, take it easy or I can relax and let go. Write each one out 15 times in succession. Try using your name to prefix it, e.g. I, Mick, can relax and let go.

MANAGING YOUR TIME

The art of time management is the effective organisation of the hours available to you. Whether it be at work, home or play, it is satisfying to know you have made the best use of your time. For effective time management to occur, the following needs to happen:

Establishing clear and realistic objectives

You need to establish what you want and why. You need to establish your work motivations and personal value system in order to redefine your career direction. There needs to be realistic objectives set out for your career development.

Planning and prioritising

As your thoughts and ideas become clearer, you need to begin making plans for a jobsearch strategy. You need to prioritise activities for two reasons: first to achieve your objectives and secondly to give yourself motivation.

Problem solving

Effective time management during your jobsearch includes problem solving. This means being able to think laterally, to find another way in when a door closes in your face. Problem solving skills include knowing where to find information, who and what to ask.

Assertiveness

Managing your time often means saying no or maybe saying yes. Your time is valuable. It represents space for yourself. Time to think. Time for action. Other people may intrude on this and you need to be able to say assertively what you need to happen. Being assertive means respecting your rights to define yourself while respecting the rights of others to do the same for themselves. Being passive means letting others use you. Being aggressive means you use others. Being assertive means self respect, valuing your time and effort and asking others to respect your wishes.

Letting go

There are only so many hours in a day to do things, to see other people and to be with yourself. Sometimes, you need to say goodbye — to let go of something or someone in order to make room for new growth. Your redundancy was an enforced goodbye. Maybe, as you review your life, there are other goodbyes to make.

Decision making

It is better to make a decision which may be bad than not to do anything at all and live to regret it. Successful time management involves making decisions, accepting responsibility for them and seeing them through. Dithering wastes time and takes up mental effort needlessly. We tend to put off making decisions because we are afraid of failure or appearing stupid. But if we make a mistake, we learn, and if we have self respect, how can we look stupid? What we think of ourselves is more important than how we believe (often wrongly) others are seeing us.

Major time wasters

interruptions	poor reading skills
bad crisis management	addiction to adrenaline
junk mail	lack of planning
procrastination	feeling guilty
travel	over-tight schedules
not finishing things	not listening
reluctance to confront	talking too much
can't say no	poor sense of time
laziness	poor rapport skills

What do **you** do to waste time?

Guidelines for successful time management

- Prioritise
- Don't waste time
- Set your goals
- Plan
- Delegate and work with others
- Manage your stress and health
- Review.

Figure 5 illustrates your time management diary. Fill this in for one day and see what kind of activities are useful and which waste time.

Project

List all the jobs you do at present. You can make this work-related list or more general. It should contain at least ten items. Work through the following steps:

1 Place an A against those jobs on your list you consider really important.

Time	Activity description
6.00	
6.30	
7.00	
7.30	
8.00	
8.30	
9.00	
9.30	
10.00	
10.30	
11.00	
11.30	
Mid-Day	
12.30	
1.00	
1.30	
2.00	
2.30	
3.00	
3.30	
4.00	
4.30	
5.00	
5.30	
6.00	
6.30	
7.00	
7.30	
8.00	
8.30	
9.00	

Fig. 5. Your time management diary.

2   Place a B against those jobs you consider not quite so
     important.

3   Place a C against those jobs you consider unimportant.

Now go back through the list again and eliminate all the Bs
by considering them as either really important (A) or unimportant (C). Now prioritise your As in terms of their importance. Start by identifying the most important and numbering
it A1, then work your way through the list until you have
numbered each one. You will make best use of your time by
concentrating your energy on achieving the A list.

$$\boxed{4}$$

Re-defining Your Value System

WHY WORK?

When I asked six youngsters around the age of 17 what they would do if they had a £1,000 cheque given to them every week for doing absolutely nothing, they all said they would go and find something to do — otherwise they would be bored. I asked the same question of six adults between 25 and 45 and most of them said they would do nothing. The difference in attitude was revealing — and a little sad.

We need to have some motivation to achieve anything in life. We need to have a reason, a payoff, otherwise we see no reason for making an effort. For example, our motivations to get up and make a cup of tea could be thirst, boredom, hunger, anxiety or the need to take a pill.

In order to enjoy our work, what are our motivations? The three main motivations are status, money and power. Status, in order to have a personal sense of identity or to be recognised by others. Money, for a roof over our heads and food in our mouths. We may have a dependent family. We like money for luxuries. Then comes power — money brings power and status brings power. We may feel power over work colleagues or subordinates, we may feel power over fate, God, the government or the system.

Work can be a drudgery if you have been doing something that does not represent the real you. It can build resentment and frustration. During times of recession, employers hold the winning hand and may deliberately create an environment of fear to keep at bay the pay claims. If you don't feel valued or appreciated, this can wear away at the human spirit, leaving morale and motivation low.

To be realistic, we are not going to be happy in our work all of the time, nor are we going to like everyone we work with, nor is everyone going to like us. But we do have the right to enjoy our work and to use and develop our skills as much as possible.

Work purpose self assessment

◆ How can I begin taking steps toward discovering and doing work that would be personally meaningful?

◆ Would I like to return to study or training to improve my career path?

◆ What are my most important values with regard to career achievement?

◆ Is material success my main motivation for why I work?

Mark the following out of five for how true you think it is. Work:

— is something I do for money

— helps me get up in the morning

— provides me with a sense of purpose

— provides me with interesting challenges

— takes me away from the family	— makes me feel needed
— gives my life structure	— gives me status
— gives me an identity	— is unenjoyable
— gives me a social life	— is boring.

What do you miss by not working?

The bridge of life

Each of us goes through cycles in life. Broadly speaking, the cycles correspond to ages and to a greater or lesser extent, we all share the cycles.

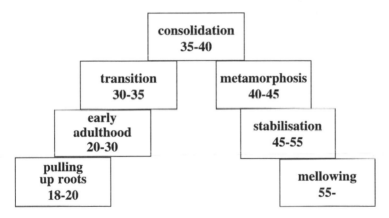

Fig. 6. The bridge of life.

Pulling up roots — leaving the nest, flexing the wings to express individuality, realising that there are different ways of being

Early adulthood — first commitments to adult responsibilities, trying out parental rules in the world, early mistakes

Transition — re-examination of parental rules,

reassessment of current relationships and career, challenges to our old ways of thinking, more long-term planning beginning to occur

Consolidation — seeking to become established, the beginning of feeling pressurised by time, making long-term goals based on our true individuality and not on family expectations

Metamorphosis — facing the chasm between ideals and reality, new career, new relationships, breaking down, breaking away

Stabilisation — increased stability following changes

Mellowing — achievement losing potency in the face of increased self satisfaction and inner peace with self.

My work values and motivations

Your value system gives shape to your life experiences. Your values are mostly in your subconscious and are formed by society and early family conditioning. You may share them or you may be carrying them around with you, believing they are your own. This exercise represents your personal needs behind your job choice. Go through the list, noting those values that are important to you.

accomplishment	being appreciated	developing new skills
activity	being efficient	gaining knowledge
a sense of community	being expert	having authority
being a success	being of service	having responsibility
being a team member	creativity	helping society

independence	respect from others	taking risks
influence	self development	to be proactive
making decisions	self respect	to motivate others
meeting deadlines	sense of purpose	usefulness
overcoming	social interaction	using my intellect
challenges	status	
public contact	supporting others	

Self assessment

Who are you? Who or what we believe ourselves to be is relevant to how we perceive ourselves out in the world. Write down without thinking, who or what you believe yourself to be at this point in time.

Project: Where am I at?

Reflect upon this period in your life and ask yourself 'Where am I at in my life right now?' Think about what kind of time this is for you. Consider the event or events which have marked the beginning of this period and think about the chief characteristics of this period. Is it a hectic time? A time of crisis? A period of transition? A stagnant period? Draw any images, colours, forms or write any words or statements that reflect where you are in your life at this particular time.

My career needs and wants

What we need and want in our work may be one and the same. What we want is desirable but not essential to our well-being. What we need is vital to our sense of self. Complete the following and find out what the difference is for you.

1. I want
    e.g. stimulation, stable income for emotional security, to

create something of substance and for a reason, to be challenged, a higher income, a sense of belonging.

2. I need
   e.g. to contribute to household expenses, to be doing something useful, to be more independent, to be needed, to develop new skills.

3. What will happen if I don't have it?
   e.g. I will feel trapped, useless, bored and frustrated.

4. What could I begin to do to remedy the situation?
   e.g. re-train, consider more permanent positions offering autonomy.

ASSESSING YOUR SKILLS AND STRENGTHS

Skills can be broadly divided into four groups:

Basic skills
These are needed for daily life and include communication skills, numeracy, literacy, communication skills, self-motivation, organisational skills and self-management.

Job specific skills (vocational)
These relate to specific types of work e.g. accounting.

Personal (or soft) skills
These encompass a range of skills related to attitude and behaviour such as time management, teamwork, negotiation skills, and the ability to explore and create opportunities, decision-making skills, diversification and flexibility.

Transferable skills
These are portable skills, which can be taken from one job to another and might include IT skills, supervisory/

management skills, customer care or linguistic and cultural skills.

Evaluating your skills

IT skills
What software packages can you use?
Are you experienced in network systems?
Have you programming experience?
Can you use the internet?
Have you knowledge of teleworking?

Leadership skills
Which of the following skills do you have?

listening	focus
accessibility	decisiveness
motivating others	solving problems
developing vision	being pro-active
setting long-term goals	delegating tasks
acknowledging mistakes	marketing
giving feedback	sharing power
promoting team effort	looking for challenges
strategic planning	setting objectives
planning work	financial management
managing resources	quality management
report writing	coaching
skills training	performance appraisal
project management	staff development
team building	managing change

Customer care skills
Do you have the following skills?
finding information
working as part of the team

dealing with complaints
keeping records
finding solutions
tact

Job specific skills
Which of the following have you been trained in or had extensive experience of (through paid or unpaid work)?

◆ Communications e.g. journalism, publishing
◆ Construction e.g. building, electrical, heating and ventilation
◆ Developing skill and knowledge e.g. teaching, training
◆ Engineering e.g. aeronautical, electric power, telecommunications, vehicle maintenance
◆ Natural resources e.g. gas, petroleum, oil and gas technology, water treatment and supply
◆ Manufacturing
◆ Providing business services e.g. banking, computer services, insurance, administration
◆ Providing services and goods e.g. beauty, food and drink, tourism, sport and recreation
◆ Providing health and social care e.g. child care, housing, probation work
◆ Providing protective services e.g. armed forces, security
◆ Tending land, animals and plants e.g. agriculture, animal care, landscape design
◆ Transport e.g. distribution

Linguistic and cultural skills
Which languages can you speak with confidence?
Which cultures do you feel comfortable working within?

Personal skills
How good are you at selling your skills to potential employers?
Do you bounce back quickly after a disappointment?
Can you do several tasks at once?
Do you enjoy working in teams?
Are you a self-starter?
Can you set realistic goals?
Are you reliable?
How good are you at developing opportunities into practical outcomes?
Are you efficient?
Can you adapt?

Evaluating your achievements

An additional bonus to your toolbox is your achievements. Potential employers like to know what you have done in the past as it indicates what you could do for them in the future. Do you have a track record of:

cutting costs	improving team work
improving the appearance	developing staff performance
of something	turning round a negative
increasing sales	situation
cutting staff costs	avoiding potential problems
meeting deadlines easily	opening up more potential
providing more information	making the boss look good

Using your strengths

Your strengths describe your personal qualities. As well as what you can do, part of your sales pitch is what you are like as a person. Underline the strengths you identify with:

adaptable	aggressive	ambitious	assertive
calm	caring	cautious	competitive
confident	conscientious	creative	decisive
dedicated	dependable	determined	diplomatic
dynamic	easy going	efficient	encouraging
energetic	enterprising	extrovert	fair
firm	flexible	friendly	hardworking
helpful	initiator	innovative	intuitive
lateral thinker	leader	logical	methodical
meticulous	objective	ordered	organised
outgoing	patient	perceptive	persuasive
practical	precise	pro-active	resourceful

YOUR IDEAL CAREER

You are to imagine that there are no constraints of money, age, or health. Identify your ideal career with details such as job specification, with whom would you work, in what kind of surroundings, with what kind of authority and responsibilities, with what kind of working day. Detail career progression and income sought, opportunities for using your present skills and developing others.

Now think through the following:

◆ What does the fantasy indicate about what I would value and aspire to?

◆ What are the differences between fantasy and my reality?

◆ How much of my fantasy is achievable at the present or might be in the future?

◆ What are the barriers to my achieving some of my fantasy and how might these be overcome?

◆ What would be the consequences of my working to achieve some of the features of my fantasy, for myself and for other people?

◆ What objectives would I like to set myself on the basis of this exercise?

Who we are produces what we do — in love, social activities, family relationships, hobbies and work. As we build a solid foundation of self discovery, we can erect a building that truly represents our inner self.

The face of work is changing. One piece of technology can do the work of several people. Certain industries have fallen, not to rise again. However, new industries have arisen and they need to be serviced — but not everyone is suited to everything.

Re-defining value systems helps to restructure the beliefs which fuel our motivation for work. As we evolve in our own life, so society evolves through its life. As we discover why we want to work and what we want to do, we can then start networking out into the community. We can begin the exciting journey of discovering how we can help each other achieve our goals.

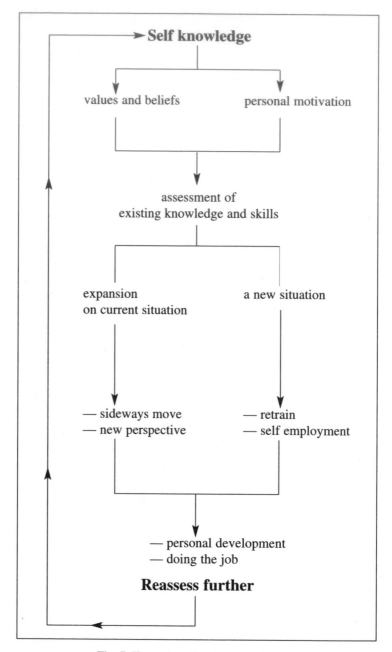

Fig. 7. Know thyself and get a better job.

Setting up a Career Development Strategy

RESEARCHING THE JOB MARKET

Economic and labour trends

It is useful to consider the economic trends both nationally and locally when researching the job market. Issues such as the impact of local and national government budgets within your area may affect the economic flow and therefore your employment. Your local Chamber of Commerce, the Town Hall and Jobcentres could provide the information you require.

It is of benefit to you to research employment statistics within your locality. Do you live in a high unemployment area? Would it be worth widening your catchment area and commuting? Are there times of the year when there are more jobs on the market — before Christmas or during the summer? A temporary job during these times could lead to networking contacts.

Keeping up to date with trends in technology

Although technology has enabled new markets and better service, it has also contributed to higher unemployment. Technology has, in part, replaced people. What happens to the people? They can learn either the skills to operate the technology or new skills. Applied technology is a booming market — computers, media, robotics, virtual reality — all steadily growing areas. If you choose to jump on the bandwagon and secure your future, you need to be aware of the development of technology in your field of expertise. Will employment dwindle as technology entrenches itself further? Do you want to be involved in that technology? Could you find a sideways niche in your market that doesn't involve so much technology? You need to keep up-to-date with developments and training opportunities. Or maybe you will decide to change your field of expertise altogether.

Be aware of the development of individual companies

Which companies are making people redundant in your area? What new companies are moving in? Are any established companies considering expansion?

Know the demand rate within your own professional area

Are you aware of the demand rate for your area of expertise? Is your work seasonal, e.g. lecturing? Do you need to upgrade your skills to keep abreast of current trends? Are you aware of new trends within your profession?

Do you know?

1 Which are the ten biggest factories in your county?

2 Which are the two biggest factories in your town or city?

3 Which are the ten biggest office firms in your county?

4 Which are the two biggest office firms in your town or city?

5 Which firms have announced redundancies in your town or city within the last six months?

6 Which new firms have moved into your town or city within the last six months?

RETURNING TO STUDY

As you do your research, it may become apparent that returning to study or re-training may be appropriate. Issues to consider might include:

- whether you want to return full or part-time
- costs such as course fees, exam fees, books and equipment, travel and childcare
- whether you want a qualification course for a new job
- whether you want a course for updating skills in your current profession
- whether you want a course to help you set up in self employment
- what effects retraining might have on your benefits.

ORGANISING YOUR JOBSEARCH STRATEGY

Setting your target job

You will need to decide:

- what skills you want to use
- at what level you want to work
- in what market you want to work
- in what geographical area you want to work
- the salary you require.

Budgeting the cost of jobsearch

Your budget should include a financial allowance for the following:

- computer usage including paper, envelopes and printer cartridge
- stationery including stapler, paper clips and presentation folder
- subscriptions to periodicals, trade journals and newspapers
- reference books and manuals
- photocopying
- telephone
- car, including parking and petrol
- other travel
- postage.

Using Jobcentre Plus

Employment Services have now become part of Jobcentre Plus. In 17 areas Jobcentre Plus pathfinder offices are already offering a fully integrated work and benefit services and there are plans to open further fully integrated Jobcentre Plus offices from October 2002. It will take several years to integrate the entire local office network of Jobcentres and Benefits Agency offices fully. During this time, services will continue to be provided in local social security offices and Jobcentres (guidance on benefits, work and training), which will be part of the Jobcentre Plus network. To find out if you live in one of the 17 areas already offering a work focus for everyone of working age who is claiming benefit visit **www.jobcentreplus.gov.uk** for the number of your nearest office. When you call Jobcentre Plus in these 17 areas you will be asked if you want to claim benefit and if you think you are ready to look for work. If you are looking for work you will be given details of local vacancies for which you are suitable. The person you speak to will take your personal details and arrange for you to meet a personal adviser.

Using the TECs

The Training and Enterprise Councils provide funding and access to a broad range of programmes for those wishing to improve their working life.

MY AGENCY APPROACH CARD

Agency:

Telephone:

Contact Name:

Meeting:

Notes:

Fig. 8. Recording your agency contacts.

Career counselling

This is a growing area of business where you will be charged for the service provided. There are both general and specific areas of counselling, e.g. women, redundancy, coming up to retirement. Career counselling:

- tells you about working environments
- may suggest possible contacts
- tells you what kind of jobs match your skills, needs and experience
- defines what skills are needed for a particular job

- recommends additional training to give credibility
- may uncover areas of employment you hadn't considered
- will challenge you to think more creatively.

Using registers and placement agencies

In general, these tend to cater for junior, professional and lower management. Some agencies cater for more specific requirements such as accountancy, secretarial and clerical, nurses or sales personnel. Charges are made to the employer and not to yourself. Be aware of being asked for money in return for work. This is unethical. Keep a record of the contacts you make with agencies (see Figure 8).

Colleges and universities

Colleges and universities have their own career counselling departments which outsiders may be able to access. They may also provide information on local employment opportunities.

Using the careers office

There are career centres in most large towns and they provide information on local employment opportunities, career descriptions, information on what skills are needed for a particular job, information on training and educational opportunities. They are primarily aimed at younger people.

Using the library

The reference part of any library is an invaluable source of information. They usually have the national and local papers for reference as well as trade directories for researching company profiles. You can access contact names, addresses and telephone numbers. A photocopier is usually available.

Researching a prospective employer

You can access the latest accounts and other financial information plus directors' names from the Registrar of Companies and Limited Partnerships. Your local Chamber of Commerce may also be able to help. You can also use the company reference books in your local library.

JOBSEARCH ON THE INTERNET

The internet is a huge information resource where you can find out about:

- job vacancies
- re-training opportunities
- job search strategies
- company profiles
- freelance work
- voluntary organisations
- vacancies advertised by employers
- online 'employment agencies' where you enter your CV into a database which can be accessed by employers.
- advice on making a job application
- job leads locally, nationally and abroad
- writing a suitable CV, a covering letter or a letter of application
- tips on coping with interviews.

Search engines and directories

Essentially, the difference between search engines and directories should be that the latter are handpicked or semi-automatically chosen sets of links devoted to a particular area, while search engines allow a dynamic search of the whole internet. The benefit of the search engine is that it will find sites that may have been overlooked or which have come into existence since the directory was created. Thus, each of these types of information source is useful in their own way and to research any subject thoroughly using the internet, both should be utilised. Some useful sites include:

1. UK Directory **www.ukdirectory.co.uk**
   Lists over 10,200 UK web sites. Employment category lists agencies working in IT, general, professional and technical categories with links to the agencies.

2. Yahoo! UK and Ireland
   www.yahoo.co.uk/Regional/Countries/United_ Kingdom/Business
   This address gets you straight into lists of employment sites in UK — just input up to 'co.uk' if you want to see the whole index.

3. Global Online Directory **www.god.co.uk**
   UK based search engine — input 'jobs' for example in the search facility and it comes up with about 50 matches, including various magazines and recruitment agencies.

4. Galaxy **www.einet.net/galaxy.html**
   There are directories of professional internet resources in the following categories: Business and Commerce, Engineering and Technology, Government, Humanities, Law, Medicine, Reference, Science and Social Sciences.

5. Webcrawler **www.webcrawler.com**
   Through Business and then Employment links, you can reach links to American job sites, indexes to job sites and newsgroups.

6. InfoSeek **www2.infoseek.com/Home?pg=Home.html**

Click on Business, and then Find a Job to find a listing of over 250 job sites.

7. Alta Vista **www.altavista.digital.com**
   Covers a great many more sites on the web than do most and has advanced Boolean search features as well as simple search facilities.

Boolean searches
Often, search engines will offer some form of advanced search facility, allowing the user to specify their information needs much more accurately. These facilities are useful for reducing the typical size of result sets from an internet search and are well worth investigating. Most use some set of Boolean operators, which allow the user's search query to be more specific. The most typical of these are:

– **AND** between search words looks for documents which include ALL of your words, which NARROWS your search. For example, you could put 'accounting and book-keeping', which would return all documents which mentioned both words, but none which mentioned just one of them.

– **OR** between search words looks for documents, which include ANY of your words, which WIDENS your search. For example, if you put 'accounting or bookkeeping', you would get all documents which mentioned one or both terms.

   NOT between search words EXCLUDES documents from your search. For example, you might put 'accounting not bookkeeping', which would find documents which mention accounting but not bookkeeping. Note that if a document mentioned both, it would be excluded by this search term so you need to be careful how you use this. **NEAR** between search words looks for proximity between the words. You can use this as in the example in Alta Vista above, for terms such as 'accounting near jobs'. It makes it more likely that you will get documents returned which really are job opportunities in research. Otherwise you could be presented with thousands of documents, which mention 'accounting' and 'jobs' in wholly different contexts.

Further guidance on Boolean searching is available under the Advanced Search page at the Alta Vista site.

Newsgroups

You can read and send messages to newsgroups such as **uk.jobs.offered**, **uk.jobs.wanted** and similar groups for countries all over the world. Netscape has a newsreader built in, choose Netscape News from the Windows menu and then Show all Newsgroups from the Options menu. Newsgroups dedicated to discussion of specialist areas may also carry adverts for jobs so don't limit your reading to groups that mention jobs in their title. Newsgroups can be a good way to keep up with what's happening in a specialist area. Observe discussions for a while to become familiar with the group's attitudes and then begin to develop a presence by asking questions about careers and jobs. Develop as many contacts as you can. Remember to thank people for any help they give you.

MAKING SPECULATIVE CONTACTS

Direct mail could prove an effective way into a company. Selling yourself through a letter addressed to a decision-maker may bring in a lead or even an interview. Most employers respect initiative — and most vacancies are filled by the applicant being at the right place at the right time. Keep a record of your speculative approaches (see Figure 9).

USING THE MEDIA
Press advertisements
It isn't advisable to place an advertisement for your services unless you are self employed or looking to invest capital. Apart from the local press, professional and trade journals, the national newspapers are a good source of vacancies. Most concentrate on specific professional areas on particular days.

STARTING TO NETWORK
What is networking?
Effective networking helps us to keep our balance and perspective. The right information, the best resources and the strongest support are needed to keep us focused in the midst of change.

Why network?
- to make a career change
- to increase knowledge and expertise in your field of work
- to make your skills and expertise more visible to others.

Questions for assessing your networking needs
- What are my career goals for the next six months?
- What are my career goals for the next twelve months?
- Why are these goals important to me?
- Who can I get to help me achieve these goals?
- How can they help me achieve these goals?
- How will I know when I have achieved them?

MY COMPANY APPROACH CARD

Company:

Telephone:

Address:

Contact Name:

Position Applied For:

Research:

Interview:

Spec Letter:

Result:

Fig. 9. Recording your company contacts.

How to network

- never ask for a job — ask for information
- keep in touch with your contact
- ask if you can do anything in return
- respect the limits of confidentiality
- be as active as you can in any associations you belong to
- be assertive
- ask the right questions
- use effective image and presentation skills
- be viewed as knowledgeable or skilful
- network by telephone and email
- attend meetings and conferences
- write letters

◆ when approaching companies with spec letters locate the decision maker and make it clear you will be following up your inquiry.

Using personal contacts

You could use:

neighbours	social contacts
relatives	friends
doctor/dentist/optician	club contacts
local shopkeepers	vet
past college friends	past university friends
old boy/girl network	priest/rabbi/minister
rotary club colleagues	Freemasons

Using professional contacts

You could use:

previous clients	former work contacts
tutors	consultants
professional organisations	customers
suppliers	solicitors
fellow members of professional associations	accountants
past employers	military organisations
veterans associations	voluntary institutions
meetings and conferences	

new names from trade journal/company brochures/newspapers/magazines.

Starting a formal network

It might be possible to start a formal network after being told of your redundancy but before you leave. Or you could initiate a network after leaving. The methods you could use might include:

* newsletters
* brochures
* speeches
* staff meetings
* being a floater
* getting a mentor
* building a team by sponsoring or mentoring others
* getting sponsors
* networking your boss
* doing favours — bank some favours
* continually maintaining visibility through teaching, writing, speaking and leading.

You can keep a record of your networking contacts in the same way as for agencies and speculative approaches to companies.

Your support network

A support network is made up of personal contacts (not including professionals) who can support you as you redefine, change and grow through this phase of career development.

My support network needs to include

* someone I can rely upon in a crisis
* someone whom I can talk to when I am worried
* someone who mentally stimulates me
* someone I can have fun with socially
* someone whom I can feel close to
* someone who values me

- someone who challenges me
- someone who gives me constructive feedback.

CREATING YOUR OWN JOB

You might feel as you do your research, both on yourself and on the market trends, that there is no job for you out there. In which case, create your own and become self-employed.

So you've done your research and you are considering whether to return to study or organise your jobsearch strategy. Whatever you choose, it should reflect how you think and feel at this point. Everything is open to change and you may find your decisions now aren't appropriate in six months' time. You may find problems along the way and you will need perseverance and lateral thinking to overcome them.

Overcoming Barriers

WHAT ARE BARRIERS?

When we have had a hard knock in life, it can take our confidence away. Being told we are no longer required for work can arouse unwelcome feelings and thoughts. We can often slip into a victim role where we believe that our misfortunes are due to the Government, God, the local council, our age or health or anything else. The barriers we perceive may be very real or we may have a subconscious need to make a barrier real in order to compensate for a lack of self-esteem. It can sometimes be easier to blame a barrier than to take responsibility for ourselves. There is no doubt that genuine difficulties do sometimes exist when trying to get back to work. But with some positive thought, a common sense approach and perseverance, we can overcome most of the constraints.

Sexism

Sex discrimination

The Equal Opportunities Commission will assist if you need help or advice on sexual harassment, sex discrimination or equal pay. Contact: 0845 601 5901.

Gays and lesbians

If you are experiencing work problems related to your sexuality, Lesbian and Gay Employment Rights can give advice, support and information. Contact: Lesbians (020) 7704 8066. Gay Men (020) 7704 6066.

Ageism

When we look for new employment, we may find that we are either too young or too old for a job. Sometimes it may seem as if there is no employment for our particular age group. Some jobs require youth, others require employees at a peak of around 35 and then there is the widening market for the more mature person.

Some of the benefits of maturity include:

- commitment
- life experience
- increased confidence
- proven skills
- fewer family distractions
- company loyalty
- reliability
- stability
- tolerance.

Salaried work

Areas such as management, court work, housekeeping, retail, financial services, tutoring and counselling all benefit from maturity. Jobs such as being a driving instructor, or a careers adviser also appeal to people of a more mature age.

> **There is an employment market for all age groups if you look in the right places**

Hints for the mature person's CV

- concentrate on your relevant strengths of character

- emphasise your skills and experience
- omit dates on your educational/qualification information
- put a personal profile after your name on the CV
- put your most relevant/recent work experience after your name on the CV
- place personal details without a date of birth at the end (unless asked for)
- mention additional information such as special skills, languages, current courses, computer literacy
- indicate physical and mental fitness and agility
- indicate an up-to-date and motivated attitude.

Self employment

Working for yourself later in life has its advantages. It can be the chance to try a different career which unlocks your hidden talents. You could use your experience to set up as a consultant, buy into an existing business or franchise or start making money from a hobby.

Overcoming literacy/numeracy problems

Literacy and numeracy problems can have a variety of sources: a scattered early education, language difficulties, family problems in childhood or dyslexia. When there are difficulties with reading, writing or maths, this can undermine confidence and raise feelings of frustration, shame and anger. Those who are in this position may feel stupid when in fact this is not the case. Dyslexia especially can give rise to misplaced labels of not being intelligent. Help is available to anyone, individually and in small groups. There are free classes in every town to cater for those with literacy and numeracy problems. There is specific help for those suffering from dyslexia. Your local CAB (Citizens' Advice

Bureau) reference library or job centre can provide you with further help.

Dependants

It may be that your role as parent or carer is holding you back from re-training or applying for jobs. Flexible jobsearch solutions may include:

◆ self employment
◆ tele-working from home
◆ job-sharing
◆ term-time working.

Possible study/retraining solutions could include:

◆ open learning (you attending learning at times to suit)
◆ distance learning (you learn at home)

Location and travel

Relocation

Relocation may be offered as an alternative to redundancy or it may offer the opportunity for a new job in a better employment area. Companies' information may include: financial and housing matters, schooling information and spouse employment assistance.

Transport

It may be that there are plenty of jobs within your specification but outside your area and you don't have your own transport or you don't drive. The possible options here could be to:

◆ take out a loan for transport
◆ learn to drive
◆ take public transport

◆ find someone who works near you or with you and share the petrol costs.

Overcoming a criminal record

If you are an ex-prisoner, it might serve you better at this stage to get into education or training. NACRO may be able to help. Contact: (020) 7582 6500.

Overcoming lack of experience or skills

Adult education

Your local adult education college could provide a way to brush up on old (or new) skills.

Further education

The local colleges offer qualification courses to both young and mature students. You could study part-time without affecting benefits or you could become a full-time student with a grant.

Jobskills

There are various government schemes (which you can find out about at your local Jobcentre) which offer skills training with and without qualifications. You are also supported in your jobsearch while learning and you can still claim benefits.

Voluntary work

Visiting your local volunteer bureau could increase your feelings of usefulness plus provide excellent material for your CV. It will also provide references, increase your skills base, expose you to different working environments, increase your confidence and provide networking opportunities.

The benefit loop

Sometimes employment doesn't offer much more financial reward than if you stayed on benefits. Family Credit is one option which could increase your salary.

The economic climate

Financial wizards and politicians are always telling us we're on our way into or out of a recession. Someone once told me 'this too will pass'. At that time I was down, so these words of wisdom cheered me up. However, when I was happy and I remembered her words — I didn't feel so good. At the end of the day, we are each in charge of our own destiny. Of course we can be affected by outside circumstances, but we can either go up or down with them or we can make our own luck. Don't be seduced by the media telling you that there is no money out there — no jobs — and all is doom and gloom. Don't fall into self-fulfilling prophecies. Understand that all you need is one job or one offer of work and that there will always be room for you as a conscientious employed person. Don't let other people's negativity empty your hopes.

Health

There is a Disability Employment Advisor (DEA) at your local job centre who works with people with disabilities who are seeking a job. The DEA is one of a specialist team called the Placement Assessment Counselling Team (PACT) that may make an assessment about the type of work you can do. The DEA runs the Disabled Persons Register, which is a voluntary register of disabled people wanting to work. The DEA can help you get a job under the Access to Work Scheme or the Job Introduction Scheme.

Ethnic origin

The Commission for Racial Equality may be able to assist you if you are being harassed.

Overcoming job competition

Selling yourself

You are your own sales representative and your marketing tools should include:

- lateral thinking and problem solving skills
- the CV
- skill in completing application forms
- letter writing skills (for covering and spec letters)
- finding the market need
- surviving selection tests
- handling interviews (and interviewers)
- networking
- telephone techniques.

Creating a need

Find the need in the market and you could be in with a chance. If you don't immediately see the job of your life being offered in the local paper, approach companies on spec and sell yourself. If you sell yourself well enough, you may make a prospective employer want to see you even if there apparently isn't a job there. If you really are good enough, they will employ you because your main sales pitch is aimed at creating a need in them for your skills and experience (even though they didn't realise they needed them in the first place).

Making your own job

If the ideal job isn't there, if you can't create a need in a prospective employer, then create a niche in the market completely for yourself and become self employed.

Need for a high income

When jobs were plentiful and money flowed, many people built up a lifestyle to go with it all. With the job market fluctuation, money now comes in dribs and drabs — but the lifestyle has been committed to. Re-organising your lifestyle and financial structure is really the only way of dealing with this problem. There is also an abundance of lower paid jobs which doesn't help to solve the problem. Family Credit may help to raise a low salary but not necessarily the lifestyle.

'No one replies to my CV/application'

When you apply for a job, you may be one of 20 or 30 applicants. When you are rejected, it is your skills and experience that aren't suitable — **not you personally**. Try again and again and again. As long as you have CVs and application forms out in circulation, there is hope.

Been out of work too long

Your CV

When you write your CV, make sure that you can write truthfully 'unemployed but doing voluntary work' or 'unemployed but attending a word processing course'. Show that you have been filling in your time productively.

Voluntary work

Doing voluntary work could serve several purposes:

- something constructive to put on your CV
- taking your mind off your own problems
- the opportunity to try different environments

- developing new skills
- networking opportunities.

BUILDING UP SHATTERED CONFIDENCE

What is confidence?

- taking pride in who we are and what we do while allowing others that same privilege for themselves
- the knowledge that whatever we think and feel has validity
- respecting our right for self expression while respecting the rights of others
- celebrating our sense of personal power
- developing power and control over ourselves and communicating this in an assertive manner while respecting the rights of others to do the same
- believing in who we are and not allowing others to define us to suit their needs.

What helps us to become confident?

Trusting others
Safe people listen and hear you. They make eye contact and accept the real you. They are non-judgemental, direct, supportive and loyal. At our deepest levels, we know what is best and right for us. Ultimately, we need to trust ourselves. Others can advise us, but only we can have the final responsibility.

Positive interaction
We need to learn good communication skills in order to relate fully and openly with others. When we can learn to disclose appropriately and are able to listen to the disclosures

of others, we can share, support and be supported.

Listening to others as they feed back their observations of our behaviour is a vital tool to self discovery. We can share our thoughts and feelings without giving away our personal power and we can also learn from others.

Most of us find criticism from others hard to take. We don't like to think we are not perfect. Ironically, we know we are not perfect: we worry over not being right, but at the same time we fear being criticised. We interpret criticism as an attack on our very personal self. In truth, constructive criticism is an observation on our behaviour — not our entire way of being. The observation may be accurate or it may not be.

When giving criticism, we need to be sure of being objective and rational. When receiving criticism, we can choose to accept or reject the criticism. We need to learn to lovingly criticise ourselves, to give constructive criticism to others, to reject inappropriate criticism and take constructive criticism from others.

Appropriate action and positive life experiences
As our confidence grows and we learn to trust our own judgement more, we are able to take decisive action. It may not always be the right action, but we feel confident enough to be able to take further action to handle mistakes.

Being confident doesn't mean we no longer experience negative emotions. The difference with increased self esteem is that we have the awareness to recognise how we feel and we have developed the skills to deal with them appropriately. Self expression means balancing the polarities of negative and positive. We cannot have one without the other. The more we numb the negative, the more we numb the positive. However, with increased confidence, we are able to feel through the entire spectrum, thereby making us a whole person.

When we are open, receptive and in control, we can fulfil our hopes and dreams. Life isn't limited and boring. It becomes unlimited and exciting, bound only by our imagination.

BREAKING DOWN EXPECTATIONS
Of others
We should work in order to satisfy ourselves, but often we work to satisfy the needs and expectations of others. Our mother might have always wanted us to be a nurse, a spouse might enjoy having a high-flying partner, our father might want us to follow in the family business. If we have tended to go into jobs to satisfy others, we may subconsciously sabotage our work situation through blaming others or resentment. Consequently, if we find ourselves out of work, we may not be very motivated to find new employment.

Of ourselves
We may have expectations of ourselves. Maybe we were told how brilliant we were when younger, when actually we weren't. Maybe we were told how stupid we were, when actually we weren't. We may believe that we couldn't learn or achieve anything when actually we can.

LOOKING AT OUR VALUES

It is possible that our value system gets in the way of us getting satisfactory employment. We may have political beliefs which could cause resentment about the haves and have-nots. We may feel guilty about earning money which causes conflict. We may hate authority which causes problems working for others. We may want to do work which benefits the community but doesn't pay enough for the mortgage.

Overcoming constraints forces us to examine our thoughts and beliefs. It is only natural when we come to employment hurdles to hesitate, but in the long run we can do no good by allowing constraints to overcome us. We must find ways of overcoming them. Sometimes we may have to accept that we cannot overcome them at this precise moment. Maybe we will have to compromise. But armed with knowledge, foresight and determination, we can find a way through to a new way of working.

(7)

Choosing a Mode of Work

The working day of nine till five, five days a week until you retire is going. As the larger social order changes and economic trends fluctuate, this is reflected in new and evolving modes of work. Did you know:

♦ flexible employment is now essential
♦ few employers predict a return to traditional patterns of full-time core employment
♦ contracting out is likely to occur in facilities such as management, driving and distribution and data preparation
♦ there is a substantial increase in part-time work and job sharing.

INTERIM MANAGEMENT

Due to cutbacks, some firms are reluctant to take on extra permanent staff. As a consequence, a new service has emerged which supplies temporary executive or interim managers. Fees can range, according to your skills and experience, from £150 – £300 daily.

BECOMING A CONSULTANT

If you have a track record in a specific area of expertise and have specialised knowledge to sell, you could become a consultant. Companies can pay a fee to receive highly specialised functions, knowledge or operating support only as long as they need it. As long as companies aren't locked into long-term commitments and consultants enjoy brisk demand, it's a quick deal benefiting both parties.

While consultants need specialised expertise in a particular field, their success is directly related to how well they can sell. It's not what you know, but how well you sell, that will make or break your career.

Before deciding to become a consultant, determine whether you have the right personality to constantly seek business from, and be rejected by, potential customers. Do you really want a job that may require you to spend more than half your time selling? And where you'll be responsible for everything, and probably be paid significantly less — at least initially?

Developing a consulting practice is somewhat like being on a never-ending job search. You have to knock repeatedly on doors to win customers. Then, as you near the end of each assignment, you must find and win new customers all over again. Can you call others time and again, and ask them to meet with you to hear your ideas? Initially, you'll spend most of your time contacting potential customers and making them aware of you and your services. To do this, you'll need to create and stick to a schedule, write letters and follow them up with phone calls. Of all your activities then, net-working is the most important. Advertising usually doesn't work, and making speeches or writing articles are no substi-tutes for personal meetings. Accept that you won't be suc-cessful unless you network, so if you hated networking while job hunting, forget about becoming a consultant. If you feel you have the right personality and enjoy networking suffi-ciently to become a consultant, the next step is to gain a focus for your business. Organise your thoughts by composing a brochure draft that describes the critical elements of your practice. By thinking through your business concepts, you'll learn whether they're possibilities or liabilities:

Your practice	What's your expertise? Prepare a general description of the type of consulting you plan to do and the market you'll serve.
Your services	This section should include a specific list of the services you'll provide.
Typical projects.	Which of your experiences proves you can deliver these services?
Benefits	A short list of reasons why clients should use you.
Biography	A brief narration of the skills, background and education that qualify you as a consultant.

One way to determine the viability of your consulting business is by talking with contacts that might be potential customers. Try to meet with them to gather feedback on your brochure draft. Their input will help you develop your business or convince you that there's no market for your idea. Ask contacts to evaluate your service and approach. Because they may already use a similar service, their advice and refinements are likely to be extremely valuable. Your prices and niche, as well as names of potential customers and their needs, will emerge from these meetings, provided that you ask.

Remember that you can't deliver your services until you've developed a client base. To generate a list, use the following resources:

Contacts. Networking is the single best method to build business relationships and identify consulting opportunities.

Past employers. They already know the quality of your work and achievements. Notify them that you're now a consultant and available on a contractual basis.

Professional associations. Become an active participant in as many associations as possible. Attend meetings to network with other members and promote your practice. Get the membership list and do a targeted direct-mail campaign. There's often a strong affiliation between members, which can benefit your marketing efforts.

Civic and community associations. Through these organizations, you can connect with other professionals who have similar volunteer interests.

Chambers of Commerce. A great source for networking and identifying opportunities in your local market.

Colleges and universities. Many schools help start-up ventures in need of specific operating, financial and technological expertise. Establishing an affiliation with one or more may lead to promising referrals.

Small-business incubators. Another great source for networking with entrepreneurs in need of specific consulting expertise to launch their ventures.

Venture-capital firms. These firms often engage consultants for specific projects, start-ups, acquisitions and other high-profile engagements. Once you've established an affiliation, engagements can become routinely available as the firm acquires additional holdings.

Banks and lending institutions. Bankers know everything about their business clients. Most important, they are aware of companies that need strong and effective management support (particularly in turnaround and reorganization situations).

The best way to assure success is by being informed and prepared. Examine your personality strengths and limitations and the necessary techniques for success, then create a detailed business plan. Finally, honestly evaluate your personality and whether you can accept the lifestyle changes. If you thoroughly plan your new venture, you'll make the right decision.

TELEWORKING

Generally speaking, teleworking is where some or all of the work you do for someone else is carried out in your home. Advances in technology have meant that people working from their own home offices can just as easily undertake many jobs that, up until now, were tied to office buildings. British Telecom reckons that there are about two million people working at home and that more than a quarter of them are teleworkers. Although there's no official definition of teleworking, it's usually agreed that it means using modern technology to help you work from home.

A number of trade unions have negotiated working from home schemes with employers and have produced useful guidelines for their members. If you are a member it might be worth contacting your union because they will be able to advise you on complicated matters, such as health and safety. If you are working from home as an employee, for example, then your company has to make sure that your home meets health and safety rules. This is not just a question of checking electricity supplies, it means making sure that desks and chairs are ergonomically efficient as well.

Useful contacts

◆ New Ways to Work, 309 Upper Street, London N1 2TY. Tel: (020) 79 30 33 55. Offers information on a range of flexible working patterns to individuals, unions and employers.

◆ The Home Office Partnership website at: **www.flexibility.co.uk**

◆ European Teleworking Online at: **www.eto.org.uk**

BUYING A FRANCHISE

A franchise is the authorisation to sell a company's goods or services in a particular area. Some pointers to bear in mind:

◆ make your own choice of advisers, e.g. solicitor and accountant

◆ talk to existing franchisees

◆ look at arrangements for purchasing equipment and stock

◆ examine what happens if you want to renew or sell your franchise

◆ investigate the franchiser

◆ make sure the franchiser belongs to the British Franchise Association. Contact: (01491) 578050.

◆ check that you have exclusive rights to sell within the territory allocated

◆ carry out market research in the same way as if you were setting up in business on your own

◆ find out how advertising levels will be maintained.

BEING A PORTFOLIO PERSON

Because of new ways to work, a new label has sprung up. The Portfolio Person is someone who has two or three jobs. I'm a portfolio person — I am a complementary therapist, writer and trainer.

TEMPORARY WORK

Temporary work covers almost any sphere of employment and could provide an opportunity to try out different working environments and companies. It is also a good way to network and you might even find more permanent work coming out of it.

FLEXI-TIME

If you choose this mode of work, it gives you greater control over your time. You would be paid for a set number of hours each week or month. Usually there is a set time where you will have to be at work, but there would also be a flexible time period at the beginning and end of the day where you could fit in your flexible hours. You could gain by having time for children, medical visits, holidays or shopping. One of the attractive elements of this scheme is that a certain amount of hours can be built up for annual leave. Another perk is that travelling is easier and cheaper outside peak times. Routine office and administrative work is most suitable to this way of working.

JOBSHARING

Jobshare is normally applicable to a full time position and introduces part-time hours. Two people share the same job, dividing the hours and responsibilities between them. Senior and managerial levels in particular are benefiting from this way of working. Another benefit may be to provide career and work opportunities for carers and those who are disabled.

CONTRACT WORKING

This type of work is becoming more commonplace. A contract differs from temporary work in that it is usually longer term with more benefits.

PART-TIME WORKING

The Part-time Workers (Prevention of Less Favourable Treatment) Regulations 2000 introduced new rights for part-time workers. The measures reinforce the Government's policy of putting in place decent minimum standards whilst promoting a flexible and competitive workforce. Two amendments to the Regulations came into force on 1 October 2002. These cover Comparators (Regulation 2) and Access to Occupational Pension Scheme (Regulation 8(8)). The part-time workers regulations ensure that Britain's 6 million part-timers are not treated less favourably than comparable full-timers in their terms and conditions, unless it is objectively justified. This means part-timers are entitled, for example, to:

- the same hourly rate of pay
- the same access for company pension schemes
- the same entitlements to annual leave and maternity/ parental leave on a pro rata basis
- the same entitlement to contractual sick pay
- no less favourable treatment in access to training.

www.dti.gov.uk

Compressed working hours

This allows people to work their total agreed hours over a

shorter number of working days e.g. a four or four and a half day week or a nine day fortnight.

Self rostering

Found mostly within a care environment, this allows team members more control over their work times. Individuals state their preferred working hours and agree a final rosta that meets most requirements.

Flexible shiftworking and shiftswapping

Shiftworking happens when different personnel do the same job after another, often through a 24-hour period e.g. printing. Shiftswapping is when employees negotiate different working times to suit their needs as long as the needs of the company are met.

Annual hours

This system organises working time on the basis of the number of hours to be worked over a year rather than a week and aims to achieve an even match between supply and demand for staff by distributing hours worked with levels of need.

WORKING ABROAD

Members of the European Union (EU) have the right to live and work in other member states (Austria, Belgium, Denmark, Finland, Republic of Ireland, France, Germany, Greece, Italy, Luxembourg, Netherlands, Spain, Sweden, Portugal and the UK) without a work permit. UK nationals working in another member state have the same rights as nationals of that country with regard to salary, working conditions, training, social security and housing.

The Overseas Placing Unit (OPU) which can be contacted at

Have you had experience of:			
◆ keeping accounting books	Yes	No	Some
◆ debt chasing	Yes	No	Some
◆ installing a system of credit control	Yes	No	Some
◆ negotiating credit terms	Yes	No	Some
◆ drawing up cash flows	Yes	No	Some
◆ cash control	Yes	No	Some
◆ drawing up budgets	Yes	No	Some
◆ estimating/raising long-term financial need	Yes	No	Some
◆ drawing up business plans	Yes	No	Some
◆ presenting your plan to financiers	Yes	No	Some
◆ establishing prices	Yes	No	Some
◆ sales	Yes	No	Some
◆ market sector analysis	Yes	No	Some
◆ advertising	Yes	No	Some
◆ public relations	Yes	No	Some
◆ product distribution	Yes	No	Some
◆ stock control	Yes	No	Some
◆ recruiting staff	Yes	No	Some
◆ project management	Yes	No	Some
◆ management team building	Yes	No	Some

Fig. 10. Your business skills assessment.

the Jobcentre, has access to overseas vacancies held on the national vacancy system. If you wish to find work outside the EU, the OPU can give advice, but there is no current system for exchange of applications between the UK and these countries. These vacancies will be handled by recruitment agencies.

CHOOSING TO BE SELF-EMPLOYED

Being self-employed is an option worth considering if you like to be in control, enjoy a challenge and have a good idea to fill a niche in the market-place. Some benefits include:

- achieving your full potential
- taking whatever risks you like
- working the hours you want
- improving your self-confidence
- avoiding being unemployed
- working at something you enjoy
- making unlimited money
- learning about business.

Market research

There is no point in having a great idea if no one wants it. Market research is the foundation for any good business. Find out what the punters want and make sure you are the one to provide it.

Some questions for market research

1 Is your target market for consumers, industry or professionals?

2 If selling into a consumer market, what are the personal factors affecting the purchasers of your product or

service — their interests, income, age, marital status, social class, family size, gender?

3 What are the purchaser's reasons for buying the product or service?

4 Is your potential market likely to grow in the future?

5 How do the potential customers/clients buy — shop, mail order, internet etc?

6 Who are your competitors (names, strengths and weaknesses, product or service, prices)? How well have they done in the last few years? How is the company organised? How do they produce their goods? Who are their main customers/clients? How do they market their product or service?

Business skills

Having the best idea since sliced bread and knowing you have a desperate market waiting to give you their money is only half the battle. The other 50% is using your business skills so that you can administer and develop your business successfully.

Raising capital

You could start up a business with part or all of your redundancy money. Alternative sources might include:

- banks
- private loans (be aware of loan sharks)
- money from local authorities
- government initiatives
- money through the EU

- overdraft facilities
- option of leasing or hire purchase as an alternative to raising a lump sum
- if your need for cash is related to difficulties with credit control, consider invoice factoring
- consider turning personal assets into cash
- approach a merchant bank or private individual for venture capital.

Costings

As part of your costings and organisational strategy, you will need to consider:

- telephone
- computers
- printing
- advertising
- furniture
- premises
- production
- materials
- vehicles
- your salary
- employing others.

Your business identity

Your business identity refers to how you will trade — on your own or with others:

1 sole trader
2 a partnership
3 a limited company.

Marketing

Without a marketing campaign, you have no sales. The way in which you sell is your marketing campaign. Ways of getting your message across to the public include:

posters	ads	sales letters
letterbox drops	press releases	direct mail
radio	TV	agents
leaflets	brochures	seminars
forums	sponsorships	internet
writing articles	writing books	hoardings

Ask yourself:

- ◆ What is my product or service?
- ◆ What is the selling price and cost of my product or service?
- ◆ What sort of marketing will I do?
- ◆ Who will do the selling?
- ◆ What is my sales pitch?

Selling skills

You have had the idea, researched the potential, produced the goods — now you have to tell everyone about it.

Know
- — the main features of your product or service
- — the major benefits it offers
- — the most likely objections and your planned response
- — the advantages and weaknesses of competitors
- — key characteristics of your potential buyers

WHAT MODE SUITS YOU?

Term-time working	Do I mind long holidays with the children?
Interim management	Do I mind getting involved on a short-term basis?
Teleworking	Am I disciplined? Am I organised? Do I like working alone? Do I like being at home all the time?
Consultancy	Have I the staying power to keep selling my services?
Temporary work	Do I want to be constantly changing job? Can I make friends easily? Am I adaptable?
Buying a franchise	Do I trust another's products/services enough to sell them?
Flexi-time	Would I make use of the flexi-time?
Jobshare	Do I like to share? How do I feel about someone else taking over my work when I'm not there? Can I negotiate and compromise?
Part time working	Will I earn enough?
Contract work	Do I mind being given a remit to fulfil?
Self employment	Do I mind giving up a regular income? Do I want to borrow money? Can I work on my own? Can I live with insecurity about income? Do I mind working unsociable hours? Do I want to sell to strangers?
Shift working	Do I mind working unsocial hours?
The portfolio person	Do I like the idea of having two or three different jobs? Am I multi-skilled?
Compressed working hours	Can I do blocks of very long days?

Fig 11. How would you like to work?

	— in what ways your product or service meets the buyers' needs and wants
Listen	— to your buyers
Relate	— what you are selling to your buyers' needs and wants
Plan	— your strategy for each prospective buyer
	— your sales presentations, telephone calls or demonstrations
Make sure	— you know who the decision-makcr is.

The law and you

Knowing the law and its relevance to your business gives security and credibility. You will need to:

- obtain professional advice from solicitor and accountant
- choose a legal form of business identity for your business
- comply with business or company name regulations
- register for VAT
- notify the Inland Revenue and the DSS of your business status
- consider your need for patents, copyright or trade mark registration
- comply with the laws affecting business premises and trading
- consider the need for a licence
- know your rights as an employer
- know your insurance needs
- pay the business rate.

Professional back-up

Behind every successful business person is a team of professionals, including:

- the accountant

- the bank
- the solicitor
- the surveyor/estate agent
- the designer
- the corporate financial adviser.

E-commerce

Is your business suitable to advertise on the web? Could you successfully run an internet-only business? This is a world-wide market, 365 days per year, 24 hours a day. Can you afford not to exploit it?

Checklist for business failure

- overestimating sales
- underpricing
- lack of marketing skills
- failing to adapt your product or service to meet buyers' needs
- lack of skills in financial matters
- boredom
- fear.

Checklist for business success

- financing is sufficient to cover the shortfall of working capital especially in the early days
- the idea and market have potential growth
- diversification
- finger on current trends
- motivation
- confidence
- flexibility
- the will to succeed.

8

Selling Yourself

THE SELLING PROCESS
(the job seeker's point of view)

Identify product	=	What are your skills, strengths, experience and accomplishments?
Do market research	=	Where could you sell them?
Establish customer (employer)	=	What does the customer need and how can you fulfil that need?
Market the product	=	Speculative letter, telephone and CV
The sales meeting	=	The interview
Closing the sale	=	Getting the job,

THE BUYING PROCESS
(employer's point of view)

What needs doing?	=	employment analysis
How is it different?	=	what is the job?
Present details	=	job description
Who and why	=	application spec
Put out to tender	=	advertise
Check replies	=	selection process
Pick two or three	=	short list
Negotiate	=	interview
Decide	=	offer job
Accept tender	=	acceptance.

Recruitment company, Robert Half, asked 300 major UK employers for examples of their more unusual job candidates at interview:

◆ Candidate fell asleep during interview.

◆ Candidate tried to take his clothes off.

◆ Candidate confessed to being a convicted murderer.

◆ Candidate challenged interviewer to an arm-wrestling contest.

◆ Bald candidate asked to leave the room mind-interview and returned a few minutes later wearing a wig.

◆ Candidate phones her therapist during the interview to ask the correct response to a question.

◆ Candidate demanded to see interviewer's CV to check they were properly qualified.

READING THE JOB ADVERTISEMENT

When applying via an advertisement for vacancies, you need to read the job description carefully for both the stated and hidden requirements. Take the ad on the opposite page based on a real vacancy:

STATED *(the obvious)*	HIDDEN *(the inferred)*
a mature person	someone who can grow along
physically fit	with a growing organisation
living locally	salesperson
prepared to work week-ends	good communication skills
prepared for an early start	good with money
holder of a clean driving licence	knows the area
looking for long term security	enjoys driving

When you apply for a job by telephone or letter and in your interview, you should be armed with the qualities they want to buy from you. So by discovering the stated and hidden

---

COWFIELD DAIRIES LTD

Cowfield Dairies is a progressive dairy with a production unit and 6 depots operating along the south-east Coast and surrounding area.

We deliver to 50,000 customers each day, providing an excellent doorstep service for milk and other dairy products. We now require additional Roundspersons.

If you are looking for long-term security with an expanding organisation, we would like to hear from you. If you are:

- a mature person
- physically fit
- living locally
- prepared to work week-ends
- prepared for an early start
- holder of a clean driving licence

FOR AN APPLICATION FORM
**contact Martin Jones,
Cowfield Dairies Ltd, Norfolk.
TELEPHONE 123456**

---

agenda in a job description, you are ready to supply your prospective employers with what they need.

CREATING YOUR CV

A CV is a sales document, not a life history and has the main purpose of getting you interviews, not to get you a job – you can do that in person later at the interview stage. Your CV is a multipurpose tool:

- when replying to advertisements
- when making speculative approaches to employers
- when dealing with recruitment agencies

- when preparing for interviews
- as a checklist during any telephone interview.

The purpose of a CV layout is to catch the reader's eye:

- Use bullet points.
- Use UPPER CASE LETTERS for headings or titles.
- <u>Underlining</u> or *italics* can be used to highlight dramatic parts of your CV.
- The CV should not be longer than two pages in length.
- Use indenting to separate different types of information.
- Create white space on your CV through wide margins (1 inch minimum on all sides), double spacing between major paragraphs, careful positioning of your name and address.
- Use the best quality paper, ivory, buff or off-white are better than white paper.
- Check your grammar and spelling.
- Make sure your name, address, telephone number and email address is centered at the top of the first sheet.
- If you are mailing your CV, don't fold it, use a large envelope instead.
- Always send a covering letter with a CV.
- Start each sentence with action verbs to communicate results e.g. designed, researched.
- Don't use more than two font types. Times Roman is good for the body, while Ariel is good for headings.
- Avoid repetitive information.
- Letter size —12 point minimum.

Your CV format

Chronological CVs
These emphasise work experience and personal history and

Name: Robert Smith

Address: 19 Chestnut Avenue
Treetown
Woodshire

Telephone: 0111 64295

Professional Qualifications:

Heidelburg UK Certificate (K Line)   1981
City & Guilds Advanced Certificate in Letterpress
  and Photogravure   1976
City & Guilds Basic Craft Certificate in Letterpress 1974

Employment History:

Ponders Print
Brighton
1995 -
Litho machine minder   Heidelburg MO 2 colour

Fig. 12. A chronological CV model
(by kind permission of Robert)

L S Fontwell
Lewes
1987 - 1995
Litho machine minder   Heidelburg KORD
Heidelburg GTO single colour
Heidelburg MO 2 colour
Heidelburg Speedmaster 2 colour
Heidelburg Speedmaster 4 colour

Eastern Publishers
Brighton
1971 - 1987
Letterpress machine minder Thompson Platten
Verticle Miehle
Heidelburg Double Crown
Tirfing
Litho machine minder   Heidelburg KORD

Personal Profile:

I would describe myself as a good team member but also someone who enjoys working under their own autonomy. My experience has taught me to be patient, disciplined and efficient in precise work. I am willing to work irregular hours and am always happy to learn new machines.

References   Alan Smith   John Black
Ponder Print   L S Fontwell
Brighton   Lewes

Fig. 12. continued

communicate that you are experienced and established in one area. Layout includes:

- **Personal details:** Your name, address, telephone number and email address come first.
- **Education/qualifications and training:** you may wish to separate the information for education and training or put them together, depending whether your background is in practical skills rather than academic ones. Set down the dates of attendance or study in date order with the earliest date first. Identify exams or other assessments taken and subjects passed. If you are applying for a specific job, list exam passes in order of relevance. List only names and school and colleges, not addresses. If you are over 25, leave out education and focus on Vocational Training (include degrees).
- **Employment/relevant experience/career:** Start with your most recent position, devoting the most space to recent employment. Detail only the last four or five positions of employment. Summarise early positions unless exceptionally relevant to the present. For dates of employment, state the year (not month). Within each position listed, stress the main responsibilities and major accomplishments that demonstrate your full competency to do the job. Relate your experience to the job description and person.
- **Interests and additional information:** Add anything, which may stress your additional skills, qualities and achievements.
- **Referees:** Names, titles and addresses of two people to whom references can be made, one usually a work reference.

Functional CVs

These highlight major areas of accomplishments and allow you to organise areas of capability in order that most supports the job you are applying for. Good for an erratic work history. By doing this, you will be able to point toward selected career directions and play down inconsistencies in past work. If you are changing careers or re-entering the job market, this approach will allow you to talk about non-paying work experience and community activities:

- Start with name, address, telephone number and email address.
- Education may be at the top (if recent) or bottom. Put any qualification course completed within the past five years at the top. If you are over 25, omit education and focus on Vocational Training (include degrees).
- Use four or five separate paragraphs, each one headlining a particular areas of expertise.
- List functional paragraphs in order of importance, with the area most related to your present job target at the top and containing slightly more information.
- Within each functional area stress the most directly related accomplishments you have produced or the most significant abilities.
- Know that you can include relevant accomplishments without necessarily identifying which employment or non-employment situation it was connected to.
- If in your interest, list a brief synopsis of your actual work experience at the bottom giving dates, employer and title.

Targeted CVs

These focus on a specific job target, listing appropriate capabilities and supporting accomplishment. Each job target requires a different CV and you must be clear and specific about your job target and the jargon used. Your capabilities and accomplishments must be stated briefly, each in one or two lines and can be directly related to your job target. Your list of capabilities should answer what can you do and your list of accomplishments should answer what have you done. Your experience and education are included but not stressed. Layout includes:

◆ Put name, address, telephone number and email adddress centered at top.

◆ List your specific job target next in all capital letters.

◆ Use the heading 'Capabilities' or 'Abilities' to describe what you can do for this target. You could follow this with a sentence such as 'In my target job area, I am able to achieve the following —'. List eight to ten brief capabilities statements.

◆ Follow this with the heading 'Accomplishments and Achievements'. Include a lead in statement such as 'Listed below are some of the accomplishments related to my job target'.

◆ Follow this with the heading 'Experience' and use no more than five lines to summarise your work history (dates, employer, title). If you have more positions to list than five lines will allow, combine earlier jobs in a statement such as '1980–1985: held other commercial positions'.

◆ The final heading is 'Education' or training . You should use only two or three lines to detail your most recent education: school, degree etc. If you are over 25, leave out education and focus on Vocational Training (including degrees).

ELECTRONIC APPLICATIONS

This section applies to any sort of e-mail application, either a straightforward e-mail message directly to the company or sending your CV by e-mail to a company or a database. You need to send your application in a format which can be read by any computer and this means using ASCII code - the American Standard Code for Information Interchange. If you were to send it as an e-mail attachment in for example, Word for Windows, the receiving company's computer might translate it automatically into a garbled mess. You can type it into your word processor, if you want, rather than use the text message part of your e-mail tool, but if you do, you need to remember certain rules:

◆ Use a monospaced font such as Courier. Other proportionally spaced fonts change accordingly when you convert them and alter any tab settings you have used, creating a mess.

◆ You cannot use bold or italic type in ASCII.

◆ Similarly, you cannot use special indents or margin adjustments, although you can use ordinary tabs and spacing —and should do so, to create white space and interest. Keep individual lines to less than 70 characters wide —the receiving computer may have different screen widths and e-mail tools, which will create a garbled mess out of anything wider than 70 characters. Work out what this represents at the start of typing your document and stick to it.

◆ You can create some interest in the document by using hyphens, asterisks and the letter o for bullet points.

◆ You then save your file in ASCII by opening the File menu and using the Save As option, name your file and save it as a Text Only file if you are using Word for Windows. (DOS text means the same thing in other word processing packages.) You can send it as an attachment in your e-mail tool by specifying the directory it is in on the hard drive. Or you can paste it into the text message area and send it as you would a normal e-mail message.

◆ If sending a CV by e-mail, don't forget to send a covering letter, just as you would in print, unless you are instructed not to do so by the receiving organisation.

◆ Note that not all CV bank sites offer confidentiality for your personal information such as your address and telephone number. You could consider offering only your e-mail address.

Putting your CV on the web

There are several ways of doing this. One is to put up your own home page on the internet, using your service provider's system. Another way to put your CV on the web is to use an agency or resume bank that allows you to add your CV to their database. They will often require you to use the format they suggest on-screen. The computer language used to put anything on to the web is called Hypertext Mark-Up Language, or HTML. It uses the principle of tagging to format the document and the end product seen by the viewer depends entirely on the tags and the browser he or she uses. You can see exactly how any web page looks in HTML in your Netscape browser by selecting the View menu and then Document Source.

There are also programming tools available such as Internet

Assistant for Word for Windows, which translates the documents you write in Word into HTML. The golden rules seem to be to keep it simple and concise. Don't use lots of graphics, different fonts and links to everything you can think of. Remember that people looking at your CV with a slower machine will get bored waiting for your site to download and may move on without waiting for it. For a job seeker, this is the worst thing that could happen to you.

The home page should clearly convey exactly what is available at your site. In depth information can be provided on links to further pages. Pages should be predominantly text and if you use images, do not make them essential for conveying your message in case people get annoyed waiting for them to download (unless you are applying for a job in graphic web design!). Be wary of using frames - they are often fiddly and may obscure your message. Don't forget to date your pages and keep checking them to update them.

You can also post your CV to one of the **jobs.wanted** newsgroups or the **misc.jobs.resumes** newsgroups. The former tend to be related to an area of work and the latter cover any work and any country.

Scanned CVs

A recent 'Tomorrow's World' on the BBC suggested that around 15 major companies are using this method in the UK. It is far more common in the USA and observers believe that it will grow in popularity here. The software is programmed not only to input the CV into the company's database, but also to select for interview. The programme showed that the computer selected the same three people for interview as were selected by the personnel officer, but the computer took several seconds to do so against the human's 20 minutes! OCR software may be unable to distinguish between certain letters in some fonts so don't use unusual or stylised fonts in paper CVs that may potentially be scanned. You should always use a font size of 10 or greater for the same reason. Always use white or very light paper because scanners do not pick up well from coloured paper. Finally, don't fold your CV. Send it in a full-sized A4 envelope because folded paper sometimes does not scan well.

USING THE TELEPHONE

When you telephone a company, either in response to an advert or on spec, your chances of selling yourself will depend on your character and enthusiasm coming across in your voice. Some proven tips include:

- having a clear idea of what you want from the call before dialling
- knowing the name and title of the person you want to speak to
- speaking in a lively and enthusiastic manner (smiling helps)
- speaking firmly and clearly
- don't suppress your body language (try standing up while on the phone if you want to feel more authoritative)
- listen with your right ear to absorb facts and your left ear for extra intuition
- listen to the tone and pitch of voice for hidden meaning.

EFFECTIVE LETTER WRITING

Covering letters

A covering letter is used when sending off your CV or an application form for a specifically advertised vacancy.

Pointers to bear in mind:

◆ put your full address, telephone number and email address in the letter

◆ ideally address your letter to a named person if stated in the advert, if there is no name put 'Dear Sir/Madam'

◆ if you address the letter to a named person, sign off 'Yours sincerely', if you address the letter Dear Sir/Madam, sign off 'Yours faithfully'

◆ the first paragraph of the letters should state what you are replying to and where and when seen

◆ the second paragraph is your sales pitch containing relevant skills, strengths and experience

◆ the third paragraph is where you indicate your availability for interview and say you have enclosed your CV

◆ whenever you put something else in an envelope other than the letter always put ENC. at the bottom left hand corner of your letter.

Spec letters

Speculative letters (see Figure 13) are a form of cold calling. They are written to companies with the intention of finding work – only not directly asking for a job. There are four good reasons for writing speculative letters.

1. When replying to an advertised vacancy, you may be one of fifty applicants, when you write a spec letters, you may be one of two or three people doing the same thing.

2. Your spec letter may arrive when a vacancy needs filling but is not yet advertised (only a very small percentage of vacancies are filled through advertisements).

3. Your spec letter is likely to show initiative and could be placed on file for the next suitable vacancy to arise.

Mr J White
Centre Manager
Anywhere Training Centre
Somewhere Street
Brighton

Tel: 01273 123456

Dear Mr White

As a professional trainer in career development skills, I would like to offer my services to your organisation. I am currently seeking to expand my contractual work and would welcome the opportunity of working with minority groups seeking employment.

I have extensive experience in working with long-term unemployed personnel giving guidance and facilitating training groups. Additional skills include the design of open learning systems for career development and the writing of a book, Thrive on Redundancy.

Should there be any relevant opportunities, I would be happy to meet with you at your convenience. I enclose a brief resumé of my experience.

I look forward to hearing from you.

Yours sincerely

Laurel Alexander Cert Ed., Assoc IPD

enc.

Fig. 13. A speculative letter.

Mrs Tricket
Personnel
Anywhere Training Centre
Somewhere Street
Brighton
Tel: 01273 123456

Dear Mrs Tricket

Re: Training Administrator

I would like to express my interest with reference to the above position, advertised in the Brighton Echo on Thursday 3 August 200X.

At present I work for Adams Secretarial College as registration administrator and have been in this post for five years. I have just completed my NVQ Business Administration Level 3 and am currently seeking new opportunities and additional responsibility where I can develop my skills and knowledge.

The position of Training Administrator with your company is therefore of great interest to me and I would welcome the opportunity of an interview. As requested, please find enclosed my CV. I look forward to hearing from you.

Yours sincerely

Mary Smith

Enc.

Fig. 14. A letter of application.

MR/MS/MRS/MISS	NATIONALITY
SURNAME	OTHER NAMES
AGE	DATE OF BIRTH
TEL NUMBER	ARE YOU REGISTERED DISABLED?
ADDRESS	

EDUCATION School/College	Dates	Examinations/Results

EMPLOYMENT Employer	Dates	Responsibilities

STATE WHY YOU THINK YOU ARE SUITABLE FOR THIS POST

Fig. 15. A specimen application form.

4. You are so good at selling yourself that you create a need for your services.

Some pointers to bear in mind when sending spec letters:

- tailor-make the letters
- the letter is a business proposition – make it professional
- research the organisation
- target the letter at a named individual
- identify in the letter where you fit in
- the first paragraph of the letters should state who you are, what you do and why you are writing
- the second paragraph is your sales pitch containing relevant skills, strengths and experience
- the third paragraph is where you request a meeting and indicate the enclosed resume
- get a meeting
- don't ask for a job, ask for information.

INTERVIEW TECHNIQUES

Well done! You have hooked a prospective employer's interest through your CV, the application form, over the phone or by letter. Now is your chance to sell yourself in person via the interview. The purpose of an interview is to collect information not on the CV or application form, to see what the candidate is like as a person and to give the candidate more information about the job. Interviews tend to follow one of two basic formats:

Criterion questioning: Interview questions are directly linked to the requirements of the job. Used in both private and public sector. The interviewer may concentrate on:

leadership, communication skills, planning ability, motivation and commercial awareness. Each area will be examined by a series of related questions e.g. tell me about a presentation you have given – what were you trying to achieve – how did you plan your presentation – how did the audience react – what did you learn from the experience.

Storyboard interview: Looks at recent work history, education and training, circumstances, aspirations and interests.

Preparation is the key to a successful interview and you need to prepare by:

– researching the company
– knowing where you are going and whom you are seeing
– re-reading the job spec and relating your skills, strengths, experience and achievements to the hidden and stated requirements
– reminding yourself of your CV, application form or letter
– preparing for their questions
– preparing your questions.

Did you know:

◆ 55% of your success depends upon visual factors
◆ 38% of your success depends upon your voice
◆ 7% of your success depends upon your spoken word
◆ YOUR SUCCESS WILL HAPPEN WITHIN THE FIRST THREE MINUTES OF ENTERING THE ROOM

Communication skills

If you want to impress others, use the following body language and speech patterns:

sitting forward
direct eye contact
interjecting with supportive
  comments
initiating and maintaining
  conversation
being polite and courteous
sitting with open, unfolded
  arms and legs
reflective responding
even and deep breathing
steady, even pace of voice
sounding sincere
controlled and fluent voice

a problem solving stance
emphasising key words
nodding
asking questions
using non-threatening gestures
using a little humour in speech
smiling
an upright body
clear voice
calm voice
making suggestions
being brief and to the point
using questions
constructive criticism.

If you want to give someone a bad impression of yourself, use the following:

frowning
scowling
narrowed eyes
turning away
raising tone of voice
a monotonic tone
using aggressive, downward
  hand gestures
withdrawing eye contact
looking at ceiling when talking
stabbing fingers
ignoring others
excessive apologies
super polite speech
excessive chit-chat
lengthy requests
self -effacing remarks
boastfulness
using put downs

fidgeting
pursed lips
shallow breathing
eye gaze constantly shifting
withdrawing from conversation
using one-syllable responses
folding arms or crossing legs
arms behind head
hesitant tone
interrupting
looking down
powerless voice
too many questions
wobbly or whining voice
shouting
speaking fast
using sarcasm
using threatening questions
blaming others.

Questions you could be asked:

- Why do you want this job?
- What your personal aims and goals?
- What are your strengths?
- What are your weaknesses?
- What is your greatest personal achievement to date?
- What do you know about our company?
- Do you have any particular expertise outside your business life?
- Where do you see yourself going in the next five years?
- What were the major problems in your last job?
- Why were you out of work so long?
- What action would you take if you disagreed with a decision of a superior?
- What have you been doing during the time you have been unemployed?
- Would you be applying for this job if you had not been made redundant?
- What sort of tasks do you find difficult?

The following aren't direct questions, but you may still get them thrown at you:

Tell me about yourself.   You seem over/under
We prefer older/younger   qualified for this job.
Give a brief summary of your   career to date.
  candidates

Questions you could ask them:

1. When will you be making your hiring decision for this position?
2. How would you describe this organisation's corporate culture?
3. What types of training programmes do you have for the staff?
4. What office automation is there?
5. Can I see round the office/factory?
6. What specific objectives would you expect me to achieve?

HOW TO FLUFF AN INTERVIEW

1. have narrow interests
2. condemn past employers
3. show a lack of interest and enthusiasm
4. show little or no interest in the history of the company
5. show intolerance or strong prejudices
6. be overbearing or conceited
7. give vague responses to questions
8. show an over-emphasis on money
9. expect advancement at an unreasonable rate
10. demonstrate poor personal appearance
11. be cynical
12. show a lack of maturity
13. be indecisive
14. indicate you are merely shopping around

15. show an inability to take criticism

16. avoid eye contact with the interviewer

17. demonstrate a lack of manner and courtesy.

After the interview, shake the interviewer(s) hand, thank them and indicate your interest. You might like to write a

---

Your successful interview checklist:

◆ research the company and know what the position is about
◆ be yourself
◆ smile
◆ ask questions
◆ concentrate
◆ be enthusiastic without going overboard
◆ shake hands on entering and leaving
◆ looking the interviewer/panel in the eye with a smile and use their name
◆ volunteer appropriate information
◆ listen
◆ don't condemn past employers
◆ allow your personality to communicate with the interviewer's
◆ present solutions to problems
◆ sit relaxed in chair - don't slouch - don't sit forward
◆ highlight your successes and achievements
◆ think professional
◆ turn off your mobile phone.

---

follow-up letter. The most important thing now is to learn from the interview, praise yourself for what you have done well and prepare for your next one.

No one can sell you better than you can yourself. Your CV, spec letters, application forms, the telephone call and the interview are tools of your trade as a job-seeker. As well as your tools, having pride in your achievements and experience will help to motivate you in your sales pitch. You do have a work history, you have life experience, you may have a family - you are someone. Remember, if you are not successful this time

**IT'S YOUR SKILLS THAT ARE BEING
REJECTED —
NOT YOU PERSONALLY
YOU ONLY NEED ONE JOB —MAYBE IT'S THE
NEXT ONE —KEEP GOING**

9

Training and Education

WHAT IS LEARNING?

Tell me and I forget
Show me and I may remember
Involve me and I'll understand

Learning is for life. Whether we attend a formal or informal course, we are constant students and teachers. Each one of us develops and grows through our life experiences and we pass this learning on to others through our interactions. Work-related study has never been so easy as it is now. There are so many opportunities to learn. I have always enjoyed teaching and training adults because of the exchange of experience and wisdom. As an adult, you have a great deal to offer when you come on a course as a student. In return, you've the opportunity to grow and develop as a person, a chance to learn new skills and gain fresh knowledge. Ultimately it is an opportunity for you to gain confidence in yourself and discover new skills. From here you can set goals for a fresh career start and begin to take greater pride in your achievements.

When we were at school, we had to learn what we were told. We may have had limited choice over subject matter. Consequently, our motivations could have been low. We may not have been good at a subject, we may have disliked a particular teacher, we may have been humiliated or laughed at. Many adults have negative memories of their early schooldays and returning to study or education can seem daunting.

However, as adults we have choice and freedom. We can set our own goals and work out strategies for achieving them. We can take control of our learning and this opens up wide and exciting fields of opportunity and discovery.
Did you know:

◆ training amongst the self employed has risen steadily since 1984

◆ those between 35–44 receive more training than those aged between 25–34

◆ employers increasingly rely on 'growing their own' trained workforce.

Education and training means

◆ updating existing skills and knowledge
◆ learning new skills
◆ gaining qualifications
◆ networking
◆ showing you are using your time well during unemployment
◆ being stimulated
◆ being challenged
◆ gaining confidence
◆ building a routine
◆ meeting new people — a sense of belonging.

Useful learning skills

◆ problem solving

- taking action
- questioning
- finding information
- selecting
- synthesis
- memorising
- observation.

Developing study skills

Planning your time
You may need to draw up a timetable based on allocation of available time for revision and consolidation. Family commitments and social life need to be taken into account. Try and set aside a period for reading each day, ideally taking notes at the same time.

Using textbooks
You can quickly get the feel of a book by obtaining an overview from the preface, by selecting a topic from the index and noting the author's methods of dealing with it. When looking at a new textbook:

- look at chapter headings
- look at section headings in each chapter
- skim some sentences and look at diagrams.

Other methods of reading include:

- 'active reading' from a textbook using the 3R method — read, recite, record
- Robinson's SQ3r method — survey, question, read, recite, review
- Pauk's OK5R method — overview, key ideas, read, record, recite, review, reflect.

The marking of your own textbooks to assist in memorisation is a good learning aid. Read sections or paragraphs fully before underlining and use symbols in consistent fashion to mark matter requiring further study.

Hints for remembering

Recital, review and practice in retrieval contribute to long-term remembering. Seek associations within the subject area:

Verbal — group things together
— pair things together
— link with things you already know
— make up a story linking things together

Visual — group things together and visualise them
— write a list and visualise it

Repetition— write out the words a number of times
— repeat aloud a number of times
— read over and over again.

Translate what you read into mind movies. Make them as clear and graphic as possible and play them through in your head. Always try to visualise what you want to remember. A useful technique for remembering key facts involves getting yourself into a state of relaxation and then seeing in your imagination the key words you want to remember being written by a giant hand. Each word should be written in capital letters with a contrast between the words and the paper on which they are written. Work on a maximum of five words at a time.

Conditions for good recall

- you tend to remember the last thing you read
- the more you test yourself the more you learn
- the more you concentrate the more you learn
- the more important the material is to you, the more you learn
- your state of mind affects what you learn
- the more you can relate the material to be learned to other things, the more you learn.

Search for pattern and structure and do not learn everything by rote. Understanding is a more valuable aid in long-term remembering. Finally, be keen.

Note taking

Why	—	for reference, revision, to restructure meaning, as an *aide memoire*, to outline essay
Where	—	in note books, binders, on cards
When	—	after reading, while reading, during or after lecture/ radio/TV
How	—	type, write, use standard or personal abbreviation, use colour, diagrams, sentences, symbols, headings, underline, numbering
What	—	main ideas, key words, essential details, sources, references.

Ask yourself

- What do I want to learn?
- When do I want to learn?
- Who do I want to learn with?

◆ Why do I want to learn?
◆ Where do I want to learn?
◆ How do I want to learn?

Checklist

Do I want:

1. A course which prepares me for paid work by helping to build my confidence?

2. A course which gives me practice with interviews and jobsearch?

3. A course for leisure?

4. A course which will prepare me to set up business on my own?

5. A course which will enable me to acquire new skills or retrain so that I can change direction?

6. A course which will help me to update my skills and knowledge so that I can return to my profession?

BASIC EDUCATION

This is useful for improving basic skills such as reading, writing or maths. It is also useful for people whose first language is not English.

ESOL

These initials stand for English for Speakers of Other Languages. The courses are designed to build confidence in handling English in everyday situations.

FURTHER EDUCATION

Further education and tertiary colleges offer work-related courses for both post-school leavers and mature students. Courses run full and part-time. Academic qualifications include GCSEs, A levels and A/S levels. Courses might include beauty therapy, hairdressing, engineering, furniture restoration, training, building or computer technology.

ADULT EDUCATION

Your local further education college is likely to have an adult education department. Often sixth form colleges run adult education classes as well. The traditional view of adult education is one of afternoon classes run for old ladies on flower arranging. In reality, courses run on a weekly basis, usually for two hours at a time. Courses are held in the morning, afternoon and evening. Often there are Saturday classes as well. Subjects range from leisure interests through to computers and word processing and go on to qualification and certificate levels.

If you are thinking about a career change, it might be an idea to consider a leisure course. The costs and commitment are low — and it might open new doors. If you are on benefit, you are likely to get a substantial reduction in fees. Courses might include massage, aromatherapy, computers, counselling, catering, art or languages.

The Workers' Educational Association

The WEA runs part-time courses in response to local needs.

ACCESS COURSES

These courses provide access to higher education for students who do not have the formal qualifications for entry. They are foundation courses and are run on a flexible basis with additional help in study skills. Some courses are linked to a particular degree course and will give you a greater opportunity of being offered a place at university upon completion.

HIGHER EDUCATION

Universities offer courses leading to degrees or Higher National Certificates or Diplomas. Mature students are specifically encouraged. Courses might include accounting, chemistry, computing, electronics and management.

DISTANCE LEARNING

The Open University

The OU is one example of a distance learning institution that offers certificate, diploma and degree courses to anyone. You do not need qualifications to be accepted onto a course and learning takes place via the TV, radio, textbooks and other material. Each student has a local OU tutor and there is usually a summer school to back up the learning process.

ONLINE LEARNING

Online learning is computer-based and delivered through the internet. You receive and submit assignments via e-mail and you can interact with students online. News can be posted to bulletin boards, tutor material can be downloaded from the internet and you can access virtual libraries. You can even get an MBA without leaving home!

Examples of online training can be found at the following.

JER Group
http://www.jergroup.com/
This site offers online courses for the internet learner in small business internet workshops, technical writing, creative writing, digital graphics and more.

Outline Learning
http://www.onlinelearning.net/
Online Learning is an online supplier of continuing higher education, dedicated to providing busy professionals with the tools needed to pursue their lifelong learning objectives. Choose from a wide variety of certificated and sequential online programme and courses designed with your career in mind. Visit the 'available classes' page for more details.

HOW TO FIND OUT ABOUT COURSES
Careers Office
This service is available in most towns and provides advice and information for young people and adults.

Jobcentres
The local Jobcentre will be able to provide information on government training and re-training schemes in your area.

Citizens Advice Bureau
Your local CAB should be able to provide guidance in the types of courses available in your area and possible contact points plus advice on dealing with debts.

Educational institutions
Adult education centres, further education colleges, poly-

technics and universities all publish a prospectus at least once a year if not more. Some institutions have open days prior to enrolment where you can talk to the tutors.

Library

Most libraries have reference sections which may have substantial course information. Leaflets and prospectuses may also be found there.

NVQs

National Vocational Qualifications are recognised both in this country and in Europe and can be transferred across the vocational sphere. NVQs are employer led, which means that the lead bodies (the official body which heads each vocational sphere) work with industry and commerce to set the national standards for competence. NVQs are made up of units which can be built up over a period of time. You can choose which unit you wish to do and gain a certificate for each unit. Assessment is usually work-based and you can take an NVQ at your own speed.

Projects

- find out what courses are available that are of interest to you and whether you have the qualifications to do them
- find out if the qualifications on offer lead to a job
- find out the job market following qualification.

COSTS AND FUNDING

If you are considering returning to education, you may need to take the following costs into account:

- course fee

- exam fee
- books and equipment
- travel
- childcare.

Grants

The amount of money awarded for living expenses is income linked. For students living at home, this will be related to the income of parents. For those who have been married at least two years before course commencement, this will be related to their partner's income.

- mandatory grants are available for full-time courses in higher education
- discretionary grants are available for full-time further education courses
- if you are over 26 and have earned at least £12,000 in the three years prior to a course, you may qualify for a Mature Student grant.

Postgraduate Awards

These come in the form of a bursary or a studentship. To qualify, you need a first degree.

Claiming benefit

Entitlement to benefit for students varies according to their circumstances, the course they are following and their income. You can find information relating to students on the following benefits on the Department for work and pensions website at www.dwp.gov.uk/gbi/5a641d3.htm:

- Child Benefit
- Housing Benefit/Council Tax Benefit

- Income Support
- Jobseeker's Allowance
- Working Families' Tax Credit

Students may also qualify for assistance with childcare costs and NHS expenses.

Career development loans

This type of loan has evolved through the Department of Employment and certain major banks. You can borrow £300 – £8,000 to cover a percentage of course fees and the cost of books and childcare. You can take a full-time, part-time, open or distance learning course as long as it is related to the kind of work you want to do and lasts no longer than two years. Career Development Loans Information Line Freephone 0800 585 505.

Sources of financial assistance

Tax relief	— if taking a NVQ — covers tuition and most materials
Career development loans	— covers 80% of course fees plus materials
Council tax concessions	— students are exempt
Discretionary awards	— FE grants
Educational trusts and charities	— usually small part-funding
HE access funds	
FE access funds	
Trade union sponsorship	— small grants
European Social Fund	— reduced course fees, allowances for childcare and materials.

Course checklist

- What entry qualifications do I need?

- How long does the course last?
- How many hours of study are involved both at college and at home?
- What is the cost?
- Are grants available?
- What are the financial effects on benefits?
- What can I do about childcare provision?
- How far will I have to travel?
- How do I apply?

10

Your Way Forward

USING WHAT YOU HAVE

During your working life you have had many experiences, built up many skills and acquired much knowledge. Then you were made redundant — but this event doesn't take away who you are or what you have done. You are still the same person — a little battered perhaps, but still the same.

Where you are now

This book has been designed to add to your building blocks of self knowledge. We have explored:

The first few weeks
Reacting to the redundancy — saying goodbye — dealing with loss — coping with the first few days

Organising your finances
Getting something for nothing — defining your needs and wants

Coping with change
Stress management — positive thinking — time management — physical fitness — healthy eating

Redefining your value system
Why do you work — work values and motivations — skills assessment

Your career development strategy
Researching the job market — returning to study — organising your jobsearch strategy — making speculative contacts — using the media — networking — creating your own job — using the internet

Overcoming constraints
Sexism — ageism — literacy and numeracy — dependants — location and travel — a criminal record — lack of experience — the benefit loop — the economic climate — health — ethnic origin — job competition — need for higher income — beliefs and values — lack of confidence

Choosing a mode of work
Term-time working — working from home — the portfolio person — temporary work — flexitime — jobshare — contract work — part time work — self employment — shift work — self-rostering — teleworking — consultancy — annual hours — compressed working hours

Selling yourself
Verbal and non verbal communication — image and style — reading the job advertisement — using the telephone — the CV — writing letters — application forms — interviews

Training and education
Study skills — basic education — further education — adult education — access courses — higher education — open learning — government schemes — qualifications — funding.

What now?

The rest of this chapter explores:

- empowerment
- using effective thinking
- giving yourself positive strokes
- improving your self image
- your philosophy towards life
- goal setting
- action planning
- endings and beginnings.

You have now begun to assess more deeply who you are, what you have and what you know so that you are in a more powerful position to move forward into new employment that more accurately represents the real you.

LETTING GO OF BEING A VICTIM

No one is out to get you. The world is not deliberately doing you down. The government hasn't got your name on their hit list. God isn't out to make your life a misery. You are a powerful individual going through a time of change because of redundancy. You don't have to like it, of course, but you now have a major opportunity to grow and develop.

There is a school of philosophy which believes:

I'm OK, you're OK

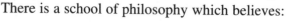

I'm OK, you're not OK   *I'm not OK, you're not OK*

- *I'm not OK, you're not OK* means I feel victimised, miserable and hopeless and so do you; there's no hope for any of us, so why bother. Neither of us wins.
- *I'm OK, you're not OK* means I'll take from you so that I feel better because you feel more awful than me. I win and you lose.
- *I'm OK, you're OK* means I feel empowered and respect myself and others and I know that you feel the same way. We are in control of our lives. We both win.

It is up to you to take advantage of every opportunity that comes your way. If there aren't enough — **create them.**

TAKING RESPONSIBILITY

You are the only person who can make a difference in your life. Other people can contribute to your success and sense of well-being, but at the end of the day, it is attitude not aptitude that makes altitude. It is your state of mind and creative approach to employment that will bring a positive response. No one owes you a living and no other person can give you something that you aren't prepared to give yourself. Maintaining this attitude takes determination and discipline and there is no doubt that there will be times when you feel resentful, frustrated and angry. That's OK. You can cope with these negative feelings — you have a right to feel and express them appropriately. You'll feel better if you do express them. However, they won't last and you will feel hopeful again. All you need is one person to say 'I have pleasure in being able to offer you the position of'.

When you take responsibility for your life and what happens to you, you are no longer a victim. Sometimes when you wait for that phone call or letter asking you for an interview or telling you that you've got the job, you may feel as if all the power in the world belongs to the employers — **but it doesn't**. You have the power. You have the power to feel up or down, positive or negative, fearful or excited. You can feel **empowered**. You are in control. You cannot control other people or their responses, but you can control your own behaviour, thoughts and feelings. If you don't like waiting for others, keep proactive in your jobsearch. If you don't like being rejected, keep reminding yourself of your skills and strengths; if you don't like not having a job, find other meaningful pursuits while you wait.

Creating your ideal job treasure map

Your treasure map should show you in your ideal scene with your goal fully realised. Place a photograph of yourself in the centre of a large sheet and show yourself doing your ideal job, in your ideal location. Cut out pictures and words from magazines. Show the situation as if it already exists. Be positive and use colour to create impact. Put an affirmation on the treasure map. 'Here I am working as a graphic designer in a light, airy office with people I like, earning good money and feeling good about myself'.

USING EFFECTIVE THINKING SKILLS

Effective thinking means taking responsibility for your own choices, accurate perception of self and others and using visual thinking skills. There are certain conditions which contribute to **negative** thinking:

Overestimating
This is when we overestimate the odds of a negative outcome to a situation: 'I'll never get an interview when they hear I was made redundant'.

Overgeneralising
This is when we falsely assume that one bad experience will become the norm: 'No one ever responds to my CV'.

Filtering
This is focusing on one negative aspect of a situation so that we ignore any positive aspects.

Emotional reasoning
This is a tendency to evaluate something illogically, totally on the basis of feelings: 'He didn't like me — I could tell. He kept staring — I feel awful.'

'Should' statements
These are the trademark of your inner-perfectionist. By imposing the word 'should' on yourself, you are lowering your self esteem. Following the inner-perfectionist telling you what you should do, your inner-critic then comes in to tell you how badly you are doing it.

Using constructive inner speech

Inner speech occurs as we become conscious of our thoughts. We can use affirmations to affirm the positive rather than the negative:

Before an interview	—	'My body is relaxed and I feel confident.'
During the interview	—	'I am calm and in control.
	—	Speak slowly and clearly. I am good enough.'
After the interview	—	'I am doing very well. I am learning a lot. I am ready for the next time.'

While waiting for a job offer — 'I am a worth while person. The right job is coming my way.'

Making choices

A further development of using powerful inner speech is using your power of choice to tune out of the negative and into the positive:

Negative inner speech	*Positive inner speech*
I am afraid of being unemployed	I am excited about getting a new job
I don't have any money	I have enough to pay the essentials
I am off course	I am on the path
I can't get a job	I will get a job
I am too old	My age is bringing new opportunities
I don't count	I count
I am filled with self doubt	I am confident
I can't do anything	I am always learning new skills
I feel useless	I do something useful every day

Preventing and managing problems

An effective jobsearch strategy involves being able to solve problems. Knowing the right person to contact, anticipating hurdles, overcoming barriers and researching all take problem solving skills. The Three Key Steps to solving problems include:

1. Analyse your problem
2. Brainstorm solutions
3. Improve on the outcome or discard and analyse and brainstorm a new approach.

GIVING YOURSELF POSITIVE STROKES

When we have been made redundant, our sense of self esteem wobbles and it is then that we need someone to tell us how brilliant we are, how lovable and how much we are needed. Sadly, there isn't always someone around who can do this, so we have to learn to do it for ourselves. We need to learn to be our own best friend. When others praise us, this is the icing on the cake, but ultimately, we need to be able to do it for ourselves.

Project

On a large sheet of paper, write out all the things you like about yourself. Put it up in a place where you can see it every day and keep adding any new strengths and skills that you discover.

TEN STEPS TO FEELING POSITIVE

1 Get rid of the word 'should' from your vocabulary — use 'could'.

2 Short-circuit negative mind-messages as soon as they start by using the word 'stop'.

3 Think about what is going well in your life.

4 Practise going from anxiety to an active and problem solving framework.

5 Create opportunities for yourself.

6   Learn to recognise what is redundant about your own attitudes.

7   Investigate new interests — try things you've never done before.

8   Before you fall asleep at night find at least one thing in each day that was enjoyable.

9   Stop criticising yourself and learn to like who you are.

10 Laugh at yourself a little more.

Remember
◆   It's up to you to take your life and use it.
◆   Nobody owes you anything.
◆   You can decide to make something of what you have and improve upon it, or you can choose to let things get you down.
◆   As one door closes, another opens — providing you look for it.

IMPROVING YOUR SELF IMAGE
Your self image is the way you see yourself and how you feel about yourself. Affirmations and creative visualisation are excellent ways of creating a more positive self image. Think of specific qualities you appreciate about yourself. In the same way that you might boost up a friend when they are down while still seeing their faults, you can appreciate yourself for all that you are while still being aware that there are ways you need to develop. Begin to tell yourself:

◆   I am talented, intelligent and creative
◆   I am willing to be happy and successful

◆ I express myself freely, fully and easily
◆ I don't have to try to please anyone else; I like myself and that's what counts.

It is often more effective to do this type of affirmation in the second person, using your own name:
'Sheila, you are a brilliant and interesting person. I like you very much.'

The anchor trick
Sit down in a quiet place, close your eyes and relax. Bring to mind a time when you felt successful and confident. Recall the scene in as much detail as possible. Where, when, how? Who else was there? What was said? When you have got the positive, strong feelings in your mind, anchor them by clasping your left shoulder or upper arm with your right hand. When you need to feel confident and positive, in an interview for example, clasping your shoulder or upper arm should re-affirm those good feelings instantly.

DEVELOPING A PHILOSOPHICAL ATTITUDE
Developing a philosophical attitude is like preparing a flower bed for new growth. Our beliefs form the substance of positive and healthy development. Our philosophy toward life sustains us through difficulty. It is helpful to develop a positive but realistic philosophy towards work, employment and material resources.

Project
Consider the following:

◆ We create our own reality by what we perceive to be true.

- We always have a choice.
- Change the inner and the outer will follow.
- Positive energy attracts positive experiences.

YOUR POSITIVE ACHIEVEMENTS JOURNAL

You may find it useful to keep a Positive Achievement Journal throughout your jobsearch. This journal will become a real sign that you are achieving tasks and developing your jobsearch skills. In the journal, record all your negative feelings and then try to offset them with positive achievements. Rule a page into two halves. On the left hand side, record:

- the date
- the situation
- the nature of your negative behaviour
- the result of your behaviour.

On the right hand side record:

- the date
- the situation
- the nature of your positive behaviour
- the result of your behaviour.

Aim to reduce the number of left hand entries and increase the number of right hand entries. Try to record one positive achievement each day.

SETTING AND ACHIEVING GOALS

Goal setting is the way we measure achievement. When we achieve in part or whole, we feel good about ourselves:

- be specific when setting goals

- set short, medium and long-term goals
- set different types of goals — financial, educational and creative
- be realistic
- uncover and remove internal barriers in moving towards your goals
- build a support network to help you
- review goals
- evaluate goals
- revise goals.

Use Figures 16 and 17 as a guide towards setting goals and drafting an action plan for yourself.

ENDINGS AND BEGINNINGS

This book is about a constant subject — change. I started my paid working life in a variety of Saturday jobs ranging from shoe sales to buttering bread in a café. The school guidance system convinced me I wanted to be a nurse, so I enrolled in cadet school but with the contrariness of teenagehood, I decided I wanted to be a window dresser instead! From there, I moved into administration and office work, moving on to becoming a professional temp working for a variety of employment agencies and developing training skills along the way. In my late twenties, I went self employed as an adult education tutor in personal development and at the age of 44, I am still self employed, although I have reinvented myself a hundred times since — a careers guidance special-ist, training prisoners in self employment skills, an astrologer, an NVQ assessor. Now I work as a freelance writer of career development books and as a therapist work-ing with breast cancer patients. But, I have never been out of

Assess which goals you might wish to consider

Career guidance
To help refocus and set new goals

Self-development
Stress management
Assertiveness training

Education and training
Adult education, e.g. word processing
Basic education, e.g. literacy and numeracy
Further education, e.g. NVQ in holistic therapies
Access courses
Higher education, e.g. degree level
Distance learning (including online learning)

Private learning

Jobsearch
CV writing
Looking for work, e.g. using the internet
Applying for work, e.g. completing application forms
Interview techniques
Working abroad

Working for yourself
Draw up your own areas of interest

Personal Development Plan
Draw up your own areas of interest

Fig. 16. Goals you might wish to consider.

Objectives	Steps needed to achieve objectives	Who can help	Target date	Date completed

Fig. 17. Personal development plan.

work. Why? Because I have my eye on the economic future, both locally and nationally. My husband has been made redundant twice, but he has got back into work again both times and quite quickly too. He's not one to make changes lightly, but he made his last job move for himself before he was made redundant again — because he could see the writing on the wall. In your working life, there are no beginnings and endings, only wheels of change as you move seamlessly from one working state to another. Be in control of your working life. Create strong developmental skills so that you can take advantage of opportunities. Have an eye to the future and see your working life as a series of stepping stones to personal and professional fulfilment. Good luck!

Glossary

Action plan. This occurs as part of the process of change. When we have thought through a course of action, we need to plan the specific steps needed to make that action happen.

Ageism. An attitude adopted by those who believe that age affects a person's ability to do a job well. Employees can be prejudiced against specific age groups when filling a vacancy.

Aide memoire. A book or document which serves as an aid to the memory.

Aptitude. A natural talent for a skill.

Assignment. A task allocated to a student reflecting their learning.

Behavioural. This term refers to how we behave, our actions, what we do.

Benefit system. The formal system put in place by the government which allocates financial resources for special needs, e.g. if a person is unemployed, disabled, has a family etc.

Block/day release. When you are in full-time employment and studying for a qualification, it is usually required that you are released from your work one day or more per week to attend college.

Brainstorm. This creative process occurs when you need to think of ideas. A time limit is usually placed on the process and the objective is to let as many thoughts out as possible in the time, without judgement.

Business plan. A lengthy document required by someone from whom you want to borrow money if you wish to work for yourself.

Business rate. This is an annual sum of money paid to the local council for rates due on your business premises.

Career counselling. This is a one-to-one process with a trained counsellor who is able to give guidance and possibly assess your career development.

Career development. This is a personal path that we follow which involves the carefully laid out development of skills and knowledge.

Cash flow. This refers to the monies available for expenditure when in business for yourself.

Catchment area. When you are searching for work, there may be a specific geographical area that you want to work within.

Cliché. A stereotyped comment or hackneyed phrase.

Claimant advisers. These are personnel who work in Jobcentres. They are available to help with any benefit queries and vacancy advice.

Company name registry. If you want to start a limited company, you will have to place the name with this register.

Concurrent life crisis. Periodically, we face life crises — death, illness, redundancy or divorce. A concurrent life crisis is when there is more than one trauma occurring at the same time.

Conditioning. This term refers to our habitual, learnt responses which form the basis for our thoughts, feelings and behaviours today.

Consolidation. As we go through various learning

processes, we accumulate skills and knowledge. There comes a time when we have reached our limit of absorbing new facts and we need to consolidate what we have learnt.

Constructive criticism. This is a form of feedback which offers helpful advice. It is empowering and positive. Destructive criticism involves putting people down via a negative attitude.

Consumer. A purchaser of goods or services.

Copyright. The exclusive right given by law for a term of years to a writer or designer etc to makes copies of his or her original work.

Credit control. Information and control of customers' credit limits when in business for yourself.

Dependants. This term refers to children or aged parents or relatives who are dependent upon us to care for them. This caring role may influence the time we have available for work or study.

Direct mail. This term is used for specifically targeted mail. A mailing list is purchased by a company who then targets various addresses with their sales letter or brochure. A mailing list is comprised of people who share a common interest or goal, e.g. people interested in purchasing shares.

Diversification. Being involved in several projects.

Draft. This refers to a preliminary copy of a document.

Empower. This term refers to a psychological state involving thoughts and emotions. It represents an assertive stance where the individual has a personal sense of power and believes in their right to express themselves appropriately without taking away someone else's power.

Essay. A literary composition on any subject.

Evaluate. To assess.

Expenditure. The spending of money.

Expertise. Expert opinion, skill or knowledge.

Extrapolating. Estimating from known information.

Feedback. The return response to your words or behaviour.

Forum. A meeting for public discussion.

Foundation course. This term usually refers to a university type course and describes a course taken before it begins.

Freewheel. To brainstorm, to think and feel without judgement or boundaries.

Funding. If a student cannot find the cost of a course themselves, full or part-funding may be available from various sources.

Goal setting. Before we take action, we need to plan our goals.

Government schemes. The government has initiated several schemes designed to help with funding courses and finding employment. Your local Jobcentre or TEC will have details.

Hidden agenda. When we communicate with others, we may not always be aware of our motivations. Sometimes we may be aware of what we want out of a situation, but we hide it from others. This is called a hidden agenda.

High interest account. A savings account which offers high interest, from which you usually can't withdraw money quickly.

Inner speech. We are constantly thinking thoughts. Whether we are aware of them or not is another matter. This is inner speech.

Insolvency. A state where the debtor is unable to pay his debts.

Invoice factoring. If you are in business for yourself and are having trouble collecting debts, a factor company buys your debts in return for an immediate cash payment.

Jobcentre. Run by the Civil Service, Jobcentres exist to answer queries on benefit, display local vacancies and advise on training courses.

Journal. A journal is a kind of diary. Not where we record daily events, but where we write or draw out thoughts and feelings about ourselves, others and our place in the world.

Knowledge. Knowledge provides the inner foundation of understanding so that we can develop our skills in action.

Letterbox drops. You may want 5,000 houses in your locality to be aware of your new fish and chip shop. A letterbox drop can be done via your local print shop who will deliver your leaflet alongside two or three others or your local newspaper may take inserts (leaflets).

Mature student. This usually refers to a person returning to study in adulthood.

Media. Publicity sources such as newspapers, TV and radio.

Metamorphosis. A change of character, form or state of being.

Monotonic. When we speak, our voice tone usually goes up and down, slow and fast, quiet and loud. A monotonic voice sounds exactly the same all the time.

Motivation. This refers to our inner drive, our reason for doing something. The reason why we think, feel and behave as we do.

Non-verbal communication. This kind of interaction is through our body only. Using our hands, body and face, we communicate, often unconsciously, our thoughts and feelings without saying anything.

NVQ. (National Vocational Qualification) is made up of several units. You can gain a certificate for each unit you successfully complete, proving your skill or competence at work.

Objective. A state of mind which reflects a detachment from emotion. An ability to deal with facts uninhibited by feelings.

Patent. A government grant of exclusive rights for the making or selling of new inventions.

Peer. Someone equal in standing or rank or equal in any other respect.

Personal profile. A short statement at the beginning or end of your CV, usually three or four sentences detailing your strengths and skills.

Physiological. Relating to the body.

Preface. The introduction to a book.

Press release. An A4 sheet sent to the editorial department of publications detailing what, why, when, where and who.

Prioritising. Putting things in order of importance.

Proactive. This term refers to someone who takes action deliberately.

Proficiency. Expertise.

Project management. A managerial term used for the development of specific projects.

Prospectus. The yearly or half-yearly documents detailing courses from adult education, further education and universities.

Public relations (PR). The sophisticated use of communication skills to keep a business in the public eye.

Research. The search to discover using critical investigation.

Resource. Stock that can be drawn upon as a means of support.

Resumé. A brief (usually one page) overview of skills, strengths and experience.

Sales pitch. The sales angle taken when selling, e.g. trendy, upmarket, cheap.

Self actualisation. A psychological term referring to reaching our peak of mind, body and spirit.

Self perception. How we perceive ourselves is vital to how we project ourselves to others. If we see ourselves as lacking confidence, then it is likely that we will project ourselves badly and others will react to this. The more positive our self perception, the better image we give to others.

Seminars. A small conference of specialists involving themselves in discussion and intense study.

Sexism. This term applies to those who believe that only men or women can do specific jobs; it also applies to sexual gender and sexual harassment.

Skills assessment. We need to be aware of our skills so that we can sell ourselves through our CV and during an interview. A skills assessment is also necessary when considering a change of career. Skills usually means work-related plus those skills we have built up outside of work that may be relevant, e.g. rock climbing, writing.

Skills. Our ability to perform specific tasks. When we use our skills, we are demonstrating through doing something.

Sole trader. A sole trader is someone who is self employed and working alone.

Stats. Short for statistics.

STD code. The code which comes before your telephone number and designates the area.

Stock control. The maintenance of stock levels and re-ordering.

Study skills. When we are teaching ourselves or being

taught, part of the process is using effective study skills which develop the ability for note taking and writing of essays and projects.

Sub-conscious. Part of the mind that is not fully conscious but is able to influence actions.

Summer school. The Open University in particular has summer schools as part of its curriculum. A summer school is usually a residential week of learning held in the middle of the year.

Synopsis. This term refers to an overview of a subject.

Synthesis. A building up of separate elements of a project into a connected whole.

Technology. Computers, information technology, electronics, science.

Tertiary. The next educational institution after secondary school.

Thesis. A document prepared by a student for their degree.

Time out. This refers to a period of time when you are not working, when you are refocusing yourself.

Trade journals. Periodicals relevant to specific trades and professions. Available through professional organisations, the library or a newsagent.

Trade mark registry. Part of the Patent Office. You can register a trade or services mark with them.

Training. This type of learning is usually skills based and work-related.

Transition. This is a term used to describe the period of change between two points. When you are made redundant and looking for work, you are in a transitionary period.

Tutorials. When you attend an educational institution, you are likely to be offered tutorials. These are individual or group sessions to discuss your thoughts and feelings about the course and your performance.

Under-pricing. If you are selling goods or a service, there is a danger of under-pricing. If you do this, your profits are unlikely to cover your costs. Also, you may give a negative image of your business to potential buyers.

Venture capital. This usually comes via a venture capital sponsor who has money to invest in a business. They also give advice on marketing and organisational structure.

Verbal communication. Speaking and listening to other people.

Victim. Someone who has suffered a bad experience, and who typically feels powerless. Being a victim can be an attitude of mind, and many 'victims' tend to blame other people for their situation and feel uncomfortable when taking personal responsibility.

Work experience. This type of work refers to short-term jobs which form part of a qualification at school or college.

Work history. This term applies to whom we have worked for, what we did and when. It is required on your CV and on application forms.

Work motivations. There are always reasons behind why we work — money, power and status being the most common. It is easier to find the right kind of work when we know what our motivations are.

Work-related. Courses being offered are increasingly being related to a working environment.

Useful Contacts

Benefits
For information on a specific benefit look in your local *Yellow Pages* for your nearest Social Security Office.

Department for Work and Pensions
Correspondence Unit, Room 540, The Adelphi, 1–11 John Adam Street, London WC2N 6HT. Tel: (020) 7712 2171 (9:00 am-5:00 pm Monday-Friday). Or find your nearest office in your local *Yellow Pages*.

New Ways to Work
Provides information and advice on flexible working arrangements, via their Information and Advice Service, a Helpline, and a range of publications. New Ways to Work, 26 Shacklewell Lane, Dalston, London E8 2EZ. Tel (helpline): (020) 7503 3578. E-mail: information@new-ways.co.uk. A range of flexible working factsheets are available on their website to download each covering different types of flexible working at **www.new-ways.co.uk/fact sheets.htm**.

National Centre for Volunteering
A resource for potential volunteers and anyone seeking up to date information on volunteering. National Centre for Volunteering, Regents Wharf, 8 All Saints Street, London N1 9RL. Tel: (020) 7520 8900. Email: volunteering@the centre.org.uk. Website: **www.volunteering.org.uk**

Self employment
The Small Business Advice Service is a free and independent source of information and advice for pre-start, start-up and small businesses provided by the National Federation of Enterprise Agencies on **www.smallbusiness advice.org.uk/sbas.asp**.

Career information
For information on careers and training look in your local *Yellow Pages* for your nearest Careers Service Office.

Further Reading

Enhancing Your Employability, Roderic Ashley, How To Books.

The Job Application Handbook, Judith Johnstone, How To Books.

Starting and Running a Successful Consultancy Business, Susan Nash, How To Books.

Starting a Business from Home, Graham Jones, How To Books.

E-Business Essential, Bruce Durie, How To Books.

365 Steps to Self Confidence, David Lawrence Preston, How To Books.

Thrive on Stress, Jan Sutton, How To Books.

Useful Sites on the Web

CAREER COUNSELLING

- Assignments Plus: **www.assignmentsplus.com** Offers a variety of self-help publications covering interview techniques, CV writing, business presentation skills, and vocabulary enhancement.
- Career Counselling Services: **www.career-counselling-services.co.uk** Produces programmes for career management. Includes training in the core skills of career counselling for human resource professionals.
- Career World: **www.career-world.com** Career management and outplacement consultancy with offices throughout the UK and Europe.
- The Connect Programme: **www.theconnectprogramme.com** Online career counselling and professional networking services.
- ICM Career Care: **www.icmcareercare.co.uk** Providing career counselling, advice, and outplacement and employment development services across the UK.
- A Perfect CV: **www.aperfectcv.co.uk** Provides writing services for CV's, letters, and resumes as well as corporate outplacement, career research, and interview coaching.
- Proteus Consultancy Ltd: **www.proteus-net.co.uk/index.html** Career guidance and outplacement specialists.

Directories

- Jobmall: **www.jobmall.co.uk** Search for job vacancies or browse the arcades of recruitment agencies.
- Jobs Jobs Jobs: **www.jobserve.com/jjj** A guide to UK recruitment web sites.
- Web Recruitment Directory: **www.recruiters.org.uk** Offers a searchable database of recruitment agencies.

Resume Services

- The Brilliant CV Company: **www.mybrillcv.co.uk** Creates professional CVs, which are designed to get its candidates noticed by highlighting their experience.
- Jobsite UK (Worldwide) Ltd: **www.gojobsite.co.uk** Offers search for UK and European jobs, e-mail, CV posting, and career and employment advice.
- Monster.co.uk: **www.monster.co.uk** Online recruitment centre for job seekers and employers alike; leading UK companies advertise current vacancies; apply online.
- PeopleBank: **www.peoplebank.com** Includes databases of vacancies and CVs.

Jobs

- 3sectorsjob.com: **www3sectorsjob.com** Specialising in accounting, IT, and sales and marketing jobs.
- AdventureJobs: **www.adventurejobs.co.uk** Offers job openings in winter sport, water sport, and more.
- All Work At Home: **www.workathome-uk.com** Offers information about working at home and home based business finder service.
- Appointments Plus: **www.appointments-plus.com** From the Electronic Telegraph.
- CVPoster.com: **www.cvposter.com** Online posting service that sends CVs to UK recruiters and direct employers.

- Cyber CV: **www.cyber-cv.com** Online recruitment service providing skills matching facilities as well as staff and job search features.
- Directory – Jobs in the UK: **www.ipl.co.uk/recruit.html** Summary of internet-based UK recruitment and training information.
- E-job: **www.e-job.com** Online job search for advertising, marketing, PR, and sales jobs in the UK.
- First Division Jobs: **www.firstdivisionjobs.com** Interactive recruitment site advertising jobs and candidate details.
- First Division People: **www.first-divisionpeople.uk.com** Features searchable vacancy database, CV registration, and online applications.
- Fish4Jobs: **www.fish4jobs.co.uk** Vacancies covering all disciplines with job news, recruiter information, and career advice.
- FTCareerPoint: **www.ftcareerpoint.com** Online recruitment service from the Financial Times (FT.com). Offers searchable database of job vacancies, CV database, career development advice, and business education.
- GoJobsite UK: **www.gojobsite.co.uk** Offers search for UK and European jobs, e-mail, CV posting, and career and employment advice.
- Goldensquare.com: **www.goldensquare.com** UK and European recruitment consultants, specialising in IT, secretarial, design, new media, and legal.
- HomeColleagues: **www.homecolleagues.net** Provides companies without recruitment agencies access to flexible, full-time, permanent, part-time, and remote jobseekers.
- Job Channel TV: **www.jobchannel.tv** Provides job

listings and vacancies from across the UK and Ireland viewable online or via digital TV.

- Job Employ: **www.jobemploy.co.uk** Offers careers in IT, sales, marketing, retail, and more.
- Job Scout: **www.jobscout.co.uk** Searches a multi-industry job database or register to receive the latest jobs by e-mail.
- Job to Suit You UK: **www.jobtosuityou.co.uk** UK job search offering vacancies supplied by recruitment agencies as well as providing e-mail alerts for new jobs, advice, CV writing, and interview tips.
- Job-Stop: **www.job-stop.co.uk** Provides a searchable database of jobs in industries including legal, IT, healthcare, engineering, and administrative support.
- JobPilot: **www.jobpilot.co.uk** Offers job listings throughout the UK and worldwide, as well as CV databases, company profiles, and more.
- Jobs Go Public: **www.jobsgopublic.com** Dedicated site for public sector jobs in the UK, including health, charities, local and central government, housing authorities, and more.
- Jobs Unlimited: **www.jobsunlimited.co.uk** UK database of jobs from the Guardian newspaper.
- Jobs4publicsector.com: **www.jobs4publicsector.com** Outlines vacancies exclusively in the public sector, both in the UK and Europe.
- Jobzone UK: **www.jobzoneuk.co.uk** Receive jobs by e-mail from leading European companies and recruitment firms.
- Just Engineers: **www.justengineers.net** Engineering vacancies recruitment site, offering job search, career advice, newsletters, hot links, and e-mail alerts.

- Monster.co.uk: **www.monster.co.uk** Online recruitment centre for job seekers and employers alike; leading UK companies advertise current vacancies; apply online.
- Opportunities: **www.opportunities.co.uk** Provides UK public sector recruitment and career development opportunities. Search through a range of jobs including health, charities, and social care.
- PeopleBank: **www.peoplebank.com** Includes databases of vacancies and CVs.
- PhoneAJob.com: **www.phoneajob.com** Offers access to job vacancies on your mobile phone.
- PlanetRecruit: **www.planetrecruit.co.uk** UK and International recruitment database.
- Price Jamieson: **www.pricejam.com** Recruitment and job search firm with listing of jobs.
- QuantumJobs.com: **www.quantumjobs.com** Offers job listings from recruitment agencies and headhunters, e-mail notification of vacancies, and resume/CV posting forums.
- Recruitment Scotland: **www.recruitmentscotland.com** Lists a range of jobs both inside and outside of Scotland.
- Reed Personnel Services plc: **www.reed.co.uk** Daily updates of job vacancies, career guides, articles, research reports, a salary calculator, CV tips, and more.
- Sector1.net: **www.sector1.net** Offers a wide range of public sector jobs in the north of England.
- Siteworkjobs: **www.siteworkjobs.co.uk** Database for skilled and experienced site workers, employers, and agencies.
- StepStone: **www.stepstone.co.uk** Offers a wide range of job vacancies in all professions throughout the UK and Europe.

- Temps24Seven: **www.temps24seven.com** Offers listings and searchable database of temporary employment services and contract work.
- TextMeAJob: **www.textmeajob.com** Offers a SMS job search service offering customers a way to receive IT job adverts via their mobile phone.
- Totaljobs: **www.totaljobs.com** Includes jobs, salary checker, company search, and agency directory.
- Traveljobsearch.com: **www.traveljobsearch.com** Specialises in vacancies within the travel industry. Including tour operator, tourism, hospitality, and leisure positions.

CAREER PLANNING

- CareerZone UK: **www.careerzone-uk.com** Provides advice and information about various aspects of career, employment and training in the UK.
- Future Steps: **www.futuresteps.co.uk** Provides careers advice and guidance services, including information on employment, training, courses, and qualifications.
- Inside Careers: **www.insidecareers.co.uk** Careers advisory service for leading professions. Lists key recruiters, course providers, and more.
- Working Careers: **www.workingcareers.com** Offers career planning tools, advice, and information.

Index